**Allow God to Order Your Steps!**

**Inspirational Stories From Women of Faith**

**Contributions from: Tonnia Cotton, LJ Garfield, Germaine Jackson, Knakita Jones, Bianca Walker**

*Acknowledgements*

Great and mighty God! How gracious thou art! You have brought me and these ladies of faith a long way, and for this, we are grateful and humbled. We are also grateful for the blessings you have bestowed upon us; both known and unknown. Your angels have guided us, supported us, inspired us, pushed us and protected each of us and our families. Thank you, thank you, thank you! I would like to acknowledge God. He is kind! I acknowledge my husband, children, grandchildren, sister and family!
**~Tonnia Cotton**

My loving and powerful God, my Creator, how wonderful you are! You have healed me in a mighty way and I am so grateful. Thank you for the blessings you have given me. Thank you for allowing me to remove fear and doubt so I can be part of this project. Thank you to my fellow writers who have moved themselves out of the way to share their stories to help heal others. Thank you to Tonnia who has coordinated and produced this project. We are witnesses to your power, protection, mercy and grace. May you continue to allow us to be a vessel for your healing love. I would like to acknowledge my mother Tiara Tingle, a mighty woman of faith, the first prayer warrior I knew. She taught me how to cope with the disappointments of life by learning the lessons they were designed to teach me to be successful in my endeavors. Thanks mom. I would like to truly acknowledge my father Edward Garfield Jr. aka Saleem. I didn't realize your absence from my life protected me from the harms of your lifestyle until recently. Our relationship helped mold me into a strong and productive woman. Thanks dad. Finally, I would like to acknowledge my children, Damon, Alex, and Karahn. Each of you has helped me mature as a mother. We have been on this healing journey together and I am eternally grateful for your love.
**~LJ Garfield**

First and foremost, I would like to acknowledge my Lord and Savior Jesus Christ who is the head of my life. I thank Him for His grace and mercy. If it wasn't for the Lord on my side, I don't know where I would be. I would like to acknowledge my husband for sticking with me during this tumultuous time in my life. I would like to acknowledge my grandchildren, family, friends and church members for supporting me. A special acknowledgement goes to my amazing God-fearing best friend, Tonnia Cotton, of Houston, Texas who organized a sister support group named "Sisters Supporting Sisters." Under her leadership, I started attending her bible studies, workshops and conferences virtually. Now, other women and I were offered an opportunity to join Tonnia and contribute to this book titled "Understand Your Assignment." I wrote my chapter in memory of my son and only child, Melvin Joseph Maxwell, Jr. May he rest in heaven until we meet again!

**~Germaine Jackson**

I want to publicly acknowledge that God is the head of my life and he's kind, just, holy, all-powerful, all-knowing and forgiving. He *is* love and for that, I'm grateful. I would also like to acknowledge my children and grandchildren. You don't know the extent to which you inspire me to keep going when I don't feel like I can. In addition to my relationship with the Lord, each of you is why I strive to get better, be better and do better in this life. I want to remind you that life is worth living to the fullest with each day that God allows us to breathe, keep going and keep getting up. Joy truly does come in the morning. Last but not least, I want to acknowledge my parents even though dad has exited this life. There would be no me without Herrise and Willie (Sang) Jones and I'm truly grateful. Thank you.

**~KnaKita Jones**

First giving honor to God who is the head and center of my life, I thank HIM. He is the source of everything. I also want to thank the continuous support of my parents, my sister and my bonus family by marriage and friends. I love and thank you ALL. To my kids, Lily, Glenn, and Chloe: mommy loves you so much and my prayer is not just for you to know how much your dad and I love you but how much God loves you. To my husband, Glenn: Thank you for being my sounding board, my iron sharpener and the man of God who leads our family with love, reverence and much-needed fun. I love you and thank you for being exactly the man God knew I needed.  Also, this book is dedicated to all of the girls and women out there who think you're in this walk of abstinence/celibacy with God alone and can't see the light at the end of the tunnel. Know that you are not alone. I have walked it and by the grace of God, I'm living out the blessings from it by staying faithful and staying the course. Trust me when I say God is Faithful. I pray my story helps affirm that in your journey.

**~Bianca Walker**

This book is dedicated with love:

To the people who understand their assignments. Keep it up!

To the people who don't understand their assignments but are seeking to recognize them.

Stay diligent!

To the people who have yet to understand their assignments. Follow your heart. God will move through you eventually because that's how it works.

# CONTENTS

**INTRODUCTION ~ Page #7**

Tonnia Cotton shares some thoughts on the importance of understanding your assignments for GOD and not from ourselves or others. The stories in the book are woven together and explain the importance of being able to piece the assignments together and how to confirm it is God, not you, designating the assignments.

**FLIPPING THE SWITCH: FROM PURITY TO MARRIAGE ~ Page #13**

Bianca Walker shares how she was taught by her parents, family, and church family to wait to have sex before marriage, but no one ever shared with her what to do after she was married. She details the challenges with being a modern-day virgin, the feelings she had after intimacy with her husband. After marathon prayers, self-reflection, and acceptance she now understands her

assignment as a woman of God.

**PRETTY ON THE OUTSIDE, HURTING ON THE INSIDE… BUT GOD GAVE ME A "DO OVER" ~ Page #29**

Knakita Jones writes about how childhood traumas can affect us as adults. She shares how our experiences in our youth fuel the choices we make throughout our life. If we are not aware of the trauma we can repeat or create negative cycles in our families. She shares how she observed her parents' marriage, the negative effect of good parents who were bad spouses to each other, and how those experiences shaped her interactions with men as she matured into a woman of God.

**I KNOW WHY THE CAGED MAN CLINGS ~ Page #48**

LJ Garfield uses a play on titles from one of her favorite authors, Maya Angelou, to express how she suffered from her father's long-term incarceration which affected her deeply. So deeply, she struggled most of her adult life to be satisfied with success, to have healthy relationships with men, and to gladly acknowledge any positive experiences she shared with her father. She contrasts the drives to see her father in prison with the twists and turns and dangers on the road of life. After many years of self-work and counseling, she began to understand that forgiving her father is one of her assignments to reverse that curse in her family. Acknowledging his positive influences in her life has helped her become the woman she is and the woman she has yet to become.

### MY ROLE MODEL, MY SISTER'S LOVE ~ Page #61

Tonnia Cotton shares an account about how her relationship with her sister Brenda changed after she found out Brenda was told she had 60 to 90 days to live. This is a story of commitment, resilience, love and faith. The whole family had to understand their assignment to help save her sister's life

### The Forgiveness Letter~ Mrs. Germain Jackson Eddie~ Page# 66
My assignment in this part of my life is to learn how to activate forgiveness. It has taken me a long time to get to this point but it started with me writing a forgiveness letter to the person who murdered my only child Melvin Joseph Maxwell, Jr.
### Bringing Closure ~Page 76

**INTRODUCTION**

I am so grateful that these ladies have come together and are willing to share their stories. Our goal is to share how we each came to understand our assignments with the hopes of helping you begin to understand your assignments. Oftentimes we have more than one assignment in life. Just like when we are in school, sometimes homework and tests would be on the same day for different subjects. The big project in one class and the math test may be on the same day and we have to focus, prioritize and sometimes multitask. The trick is understanding the assignments and understanding how to decide the order to complete the tasks.

The purpose of our coming together is not only to share our stories with you and help heal some soft spots in our histories, but to also share the common goal. The common goal is recognizing the individual assignments from GOD when they are presented to us throughout life. The stories we share shed light on understanding the assignment as parents, as children, as adults, as professionals and much more.

~ One author will share about how her son was murdered by his girlfriend…
~ Another author will share how she found herself feeling rejected after she waited until marriage to have sexual intercourse…
~ The next author will share how she finally forgave her father for his absence during her childhood because of his 27-year imprisonment…
~ Then a woman of God shares how being treated as special because of her beauty during her youth and teen years impacted her adult decision-making process with finding a good husband…

The stories are woven together and explain the importance of being able to piece the assignments together and how to confirm it is God, not you, designating the assignments.

**Tonnia's Tips on Assignments**

Too often in life we get confused by personal assignments mistaking them for God's assignment. In my experience when I take on assignments that I have not prayed about, it often backfires and I get my feelings hurt. I take on sleepless nights filled with worrying about matters that are not any of my business.

When we take on assignments not designated by God they can look like they belong to us. They come in many forms: children, spouses, family members, coworkers, friends, associates, situations, illness, accidents and experiences.

As a mother I had to learn my help may not be needed or wanted even though I desired to give it. When raising my children one of the hardest things for me to do was not give advice, not step in the lane or not take over a situation. I had to tell myself "Stop it." I was driving myself crazy.

When my kids were school-aged or less I had so much influence on them. This was the time to pray about my assignment to teach them. I was too focused on what other people thought. The question of the year is what did I teach them? There are important things to teach. Teach your children about God, share with them how Jesus died on the cross for us and share the truth about who God is in your life. Then there is the respect part, where common manners like respecting adults, not talking over people, sharing and just being kind to people are taught. And the importance of standing up for what is right is just as important.

Then when your children reach that middle school age it gets harder, folks. Your parental assignment comes with competition. Your child starts hearing the opinions of others and your voice begins to sound annoying. Trust me; you have to be prayed-up and a good listener. Your assignment may be taking on being the "Team Mom" at the house where everyone hangs out. You may even be the Uber driver for everyone. Wait before you say, "Not me." Let me explain why this assignment is not bad. You get to hear and see more. Your kids' friends may see you as the go-to parent. Yes, the parent your kids' friends share stuff with when things are not going well. You may be the parent that when folks stay over they know you're going to church on Sunday morning. Your assignment may get them closer to a relationship with God. Be prayerful because rarely are assignments easy or convenient. I had the awesome assignment of telling young people about Jesus.

Your assignment for your adult child will change. Whew, child! This may be the hardest assignment as a parent. You have to pray about asking the right questions and not crossing over lanes. Your relationship as an advisor is more important than you fussing and using all your energy to get something off your chest. Your assignment as a parent is to pray harder and be factual. Yes, it's you who gave birth to this child, but your child belongs to the Lord. Mothers are the vessels through which they come to life. Children are not ours to own, they are manifestations of God, our Father.

As a parent to an adult child, there is a lot of praying that takes place too, but it is different from childhood. It's more about direction and sessions. As a parent to an adult you want to let go but you may think it's your assignment to handle things that your adult child should be figuring out or handling for themselves. For example, you may have the guilty syndrome which can cause you to do desperate things. Stop it! Get you a good journal to write in and create a page for each item. The items may be financial, personal solutions, or business. Write what you have given to your adult child and start praying as you review the list for what you need to stop. Pray! Keep praying. Stay prayerful. Then ask God to help you set healthy boundaries.

The assignment as a wife. When you understand your assignment from Proverbs 31: 28-30, you understand that you don't need a title, the scriptures said they called you blessed. The scripture does not share that as wives, moms and leaders in the community, we should toot our own horn. It reads, "They called her blessed." That means your work speaks for itself. You do not have to recognize yourself or toot your own horn. Remember, even if no one else sees you, God always sees you!

Let's take Proverbs 31:29-30! That scripture is truly speaking to your assignment~28: Her children arise and call her blessed; her husband also, and he praises her. 29: "Many women do noble things, but you surpass them all."

30: "Charm is deceptive, and beauty is fleeting; but a woman who fears the Lord is to be praised."

Your assignment may consist of being a single mom. Not necessarily by want, but based more on decisions you made. The days when you're feeling defeated don't lash-out, go to God in prayer. You can journal your thoughts, but run your race (Hebrews 12:1). When you receive an assignment (single mom assignment) you tackle it head-on, pray and focus. Do not overthink the assignment, trust God. You need to cry it out; but get up and tell Satan, "You thought you had me, but do you know my Heavenly Father? He provides!" In my lifetime the single moms that focus on the Lord, take care of themselves and choose not to focus on what they don't have or who is not doing something, God opens doors!

Single moms, it is not your assignment to talk bad about the man you allowed inside your sacred space. He is the father of your child or children. What does the negative talk say about you? What does it say about your choices, your decision-making process? Do you know when we speak negatively about the men that father our children we create all kinds of issues for the entire family? You can't speak negatively of your kid's father without speaking negatively of yourself. Do you get that? Moms, please don't take on the assignment of belittling the father of your kids. Allow circumstances to show your children what they need to see about their father. You can be the soft landing place of love.

God promises to provide what we need (Philippians 4:19, Matthew 6:31-32). He created the universe and gives food to every living thing — including you and me. The same God who provides food for the animals will not allow us to go without (Psalm 145:15-16, Luke 12:24-26).

Regarding the assignment of being the person that is always trying to help someone and then you feel used, the question is more about what did you do before you tried helping that person or moving to the position of "little g"? Yes, you are acting like God because you want to be the help and be in control. Then you get hurt, frustrated and confused when you aren't recognized for doing something that was not your assignment.

Wait, let's talk about the friend assignment. How interesting is this topic? We must realize that our assignment as a friend may be for a season. Yes, there are friendships that last a lifetime and there are friendships that have specific seasons. Pray and ask God to help you understand how he sees your friend in your life. Remember, do not ever put anyone before Jesus! That means your friend is a friend and that friend is not your assignment. You know if the person is your assignment by how you help and when you help. Your help should not always be frustrating or a struggle. You should not be totally drained when you help this friend. There should be a time when you are sharing who Jesus is and what he can do. There should be a time of development and growth. You have to let the person go and release. Yes, release them to the world.

Too often in life, we are taking on what we think is our assignment when it's actually God's work. It may not be your assignment from God. It may be that you gave yourself an assignment. You will go through so much turmoil taking on assignments from yourself; inserting yourself in places not designed for you.

Then, we are self-centered versus being God-centered, and we will find ourselves getting upset when things don't go the way we wanted versus being God-centered and understanding the lesson or the opportunity.

*Flipping The Switch: From Purity to Marriage~ Bianca Walker*

My Assignment was to WAIT for marriage to have sex. Check. Marry the man I love. Check. Buy a nice home in a decent school district. Check. Have beautiful babies. Check. Check. Check. I'm here with my white picket fence American dream, carefully curated by my parents, my church members and other family members who co-signed on abstinence by waiting for marriage to prevent unplanned pregnancy and STDs, just to name a few. But now that I am here, what do I do when it comes to making love with my husband?

Nowhere have I found women or anyone for that matter, tell you what you do after or how you might expect to feel after you have waited this whole time. Whether you were pure and waited for marriage or just waited to have sex. Yes, there is a difference - you can do other intimate acts but not actually have intercourse and you still technically would be a virgin. If you are pure,
there is NO sexual activity at all until marriage. Either way, what on earth prepares you for a penis to enter your vagina?

Sorry if that was too vulgar for some for the saints in the back. But if you know me, you know that I am probably one of the least "vulgar" people you'd meet, least likely to offend anyone because I'm always trying to be overly considerate to everyone. Making sure everyone is always comfortable, all while having a smile on my face. Not that it's not me either, but that day just isn't today, so they will just have to get over it. Sorry not sorry. If you grew up anything similar to the way I did in the "girls are to be seen and not heard" era, you'll know what I mean. So, I write this story because sex itself shouldn't be an uncomfortable topic. Sex is not a dirty word. How society manipulates sex can be quite offensive. THEY made it a dirty word. But, sex is a necessary part of life, so human beings do not become extinct. Humans have a whole-body
system dedicated to sex for reproduction and pleasure. So how can God say, "be fruitful and multiply" (Gen. 1:28) but it still brings on a negative connotation? We can't talk about it, or should I say we don't talk about it. Don't get me wrong; I know that it's best to wait

until marriage to have sex because children need both parents that are equally committed and grounded by God's word, purpose, and covenant. It protects your heart when you are giving yourself fully to one person who is in a commitment with God to do the same. I trusted God's word to guide me to my future husband and with my future family. I tried my best to be diligent, patient, and obedient. It was not easy.

Temptation is everywhere. It's on social media, it's in your friend group, it's on TV, and in music. It's the cute guy who finally notices you but is more touchy-feely than you want or the guy who only sees you as a friend because you won't do more.

With some of these instances, I'm not going to lie to you and say I passed every test. I did not, I kissed, I might have crossed a few bases, but I knew I couldn't have sex before marriage. So unfortunately, I was not pure when I

got married to my husband, but I was a virgin. The only person I had sexual intercourse with was my husband, on my wedding night.

I'm sharing this to be real, to be honest, and to process the challenges I had because back then there weren't a lot of people that were honest with me. There weren't a lot of people on this journey with me. I was grateful to begin my 18 + young adult years in a friend group where most of my friends were still virgins and some were actively waiting for marriage like me. But as I got

closer to college, that group became smaller and smaller. In my immediate circle, it went down from 4 or 5 of us, to 2 of us waiting for marriage our senior year of college. It became harder and harder to fight the temptation of waiting, to just go ahead and get it over with. I just wanted to be loved so badly, so hung up on wanting that "hopeless romantic" type love. I just wanted the physical sensations to stop and the societal pressure to stop. I felt like everyone was doing something and leaving me out of it. Then there were all the annoying comments, "Girl, I don't know who you're going to find in college that either is still a virgin or won't want to have sex. That's impossible!" or "You just might as well stay single because that doesn't even make sense to wait that long!" or "How will you know if you're sexually compatible with someone if you don't try him out first" and "He can't actually show you that he loves you without sex, so how will you know he really loves you?" The

14

one I heard the most, "Well bae said he's ready to go, so you know what that means!!
…well, everyone except Be, you don't know anything about that"

Ugghh! I was the joke, and I was tired of waiting, tired of missing out on what seemed like love, missing out on my person. When is my person going to come? Because apparently, the love wasn't as accessible as I thought it would be.

When the semester ended, I went back home emotionally exhausted.  I started back attending my young adult Bible study and guess what our topic was? "What do we want our future spouse to look like?" Yup, God was definitely in the mix on that one. Going to that bible study helped

adjust my perspective. So, I finally wrote it down, in detail, as instructed by our ministry leader, everything I wanted in a future spouse. I wrote it down, prayed over it, and gave it over to God. I literally added in there "Okay Lord, I don't know what this man will look like or if I thought of everything, but I trust you'll fill in the blanks, alright God, it's on you now. I literally can't take

this on myself anymore." The summer at home rejuvenated me and I was ready to go back to school. I got back to school, hunkered down, joined different organizations to get more involved on campus. Then a good friend became something more…a new journey was in store.

**My First Real Boyfriend**

Whew Chile, I was head over heels for this guy. What I remember most from our relationship is how much we laughed together. I felt like we were always joking around with one another, and it helped that we nurtured a good friendship first. We went everywhere together. Every event, every party, organization activity, laughing each step of the way. He respected that I wanted to wait until marriage, I believe a part of him looked up to me for it. However, I still slept over and one thing led to another, and I had to keep enforcing my boundary about sex. Even though he knew my conviction was strong, I think in the back of his mind he was kind of hoping today might be the day she changes her mind and I'll be ready, right here. He never tried to manipulate me, he never forced me or made me feel bad for saying no. However, he was dealing with his

own "needs" and was confused by my mixed signals. I can own up to it now that I understand more. I was curious so we explored sensuality, but I was NOT changing my mind about having sex. After a few months he ended the relationship. The day he broke up with me, I felt my heart shatter into a million pieces. I couldn't understand what he meant at the time, but he told me that he felt like it was unfair that I kept leading him on like I would have sex but always shut it down. At first, I thought, okay you knew I was waiting.

You knew that I didn't want to have sex no matter what other sexual stuff we were doing, so that's on you and not on me. However, now, I understand that that's where the purity side of virginity comes into play. Exploring my sensuality with someone who wasn't my husband caused too many mixed signals, too many heightened emotions and it's not fair to anyone in the

equation. It makes the virginity journey that much harder and more likely to fail.

Looking back, I wish I could apologize to him for confusing him, for my part in blurring the lines, but I just didn't and couldn't see it then. I really thought c'mon this must be it! I'm almost done with college, and this was supposed to be the guy...my guy. But he wasn't, he was the preface, and

now I understand that was okay. I needed someone truly on this journey with me so we can hold one another accountable together. It took me a while to get there though…honestly a full two years before I truly got over him. I had to start a healing process and get back on track.

However, my faith was starting to shake because I felt like God was telling me that this was the guy, and it wasn't. Also, if I heard that incorrectly, what else did I think He told me but in reality, He didn't? These thoughts took a toll on me and my grades started slipping, and I ended up getting on academic probation. Missing tests, quizzes, assignments, and I just didn't care at

this point. I was so focused on my boyfriend at the time, that I didn't realize until now how much I actually HATED my accounting classes. They weren't interesting to me, I wasn't motivated to learn more, nothing. I just wanted to throw away the whole semester and never look back. It just seemed like it was one thing after another, areas of my life where I felt like I was rejected and a

failure. Worst of all, I felt far away from God's voice.

I went to a really dark place during this time in my life. Yes, feeling rejected from a guy hurt but nothing hurts like feeling distant from God and His voice. With the help of some good friends, dragging me out of bed and telling me to stay out of my dorm and soak up some Vitamin D, then go to counseling. I'm so grateful to them for that. Pay attention to your friends, check on them if

they've been inside too long, they might be going somewhere unhealthy mentally. The longer they stay there, the harder it is to get out of it. Counseling really helped. It helped me understand that I was just overwhelmed with everything in my life snowballing on top of one another. I was just losing control, direction, and purpose. Even when suicidal thoughts arose, which I never acted on, the simple fact that I let them stay and fester in my head was not good. It just showed me how much I needed someone professional to talk to. Plus, it was hard to talk to close people around me or the adults in my life because for someone who had great parents, in college, had food in the fridge, who am I to talk about being depressed? So, to talk to someone, an outside

party who didn't judge me or compare my situation with someone who "had it worse" it really helped to talk my feelings out. So, with a combination of me taking back control of my life by putting God back into the drive's seat of my life by starting to get back into the word of God, and counseling to talk through the initial feelings I had, I finally felt like things were back on track.

Within the next couple years after my breakup, my college major redirected, the road bump in my walk with God. I was doing a lot better. I changed my major and was truly taking care of myself. I told myself I would be different in my next relationship, to take things slow and truly

see if God wanted him in my life or not. By checking in the beginning, not after I've already fallen for him. Also, to go back to my list I prayed over. I felt like I just skimmed it in my

last relationship, but I forgot that list was a prayer I gave over to God. It was a prayer I was looking for Him to answer back then and it should be something I'm looking for Him to answer now. He said in Matthew 7:7-8, to keep on asking and that's exactly what I had to do. Ask and believe. I
either believe what He says and who He says He is, or I don't. Simple as that.

So, while I was in my waiting season, I focused on me, my classes, my organizations, just being the best me I could be. Because we always talk about what we want in a spouse but sometimes we don't think of the
asset God is making within us to be for that person. If you are God's child, so is he. If you want to have a God-fearing spouse, YOU need to be a God-fearing spouse. Everything you're asking him to be, you need to be too. Now did every decision I make in my waiting season I make with my husband in mind? NO! I asked for what I wanted, trusted His will for my life, and let God to
do the rest. I mean, it could have been in God's will for me to be single but either way I needed to make sure I was doing everything I could to be the best me, physically, mentally, emotionally, and spiritually, to be the healthiest version of me. Which benefited me and God's kingdom either way. Some of the things I did for example, whenever I would get lonely, I would just go on what I call a "Date with Jesus." Whatever I wanted from my dating life, I would just replace the guy with Jesus. I went on picnic dates with Jesus, sometimes double dates with my good friend and Christian accountability friend, Annie. I had to surround myself with people that were going in the same direction I was going. I had to stay focused on the goal: growth in my walk with God,
my upcoming graduation, and my future career.

But man, I'll never forget the day I officially got over my ex. I had just come from a fraternity party and I saw him there and we chatted for a bit and planned to hang out at my apartment afterwards. It was harmless and we did all the time as friends, an actual Netflix and chill! However, I'm not going to lie and say it didn't cross my mind, more than a friend thought, wondering if I still had feelings for him and him for me.

We were watching Sister, Sister laughing, and I was laying on my bed with a blanket and he was sitting across the room in my office chair and for a second, I just looked over at him watching the episode and right at that

moment, it hit me. "Wow. I'm really over this guy. I feel nothing BUT friendship." I was shocked with myself. Everything I went through, emotionally because of this guy, it's like it was gone. That's something only God can do. It's like he took the pain from it all and just left all the life's lessons that I needed to learn for the next step, and the next relationship.

That night I saw my ex after the fraternity party was Thursday of homecoming weekend, and here comes the following Monday. My first class of the morning ended up being canceled and I had a marketing test in a couple of hours, so I decided to go into one of the study rooms to

review a few last-minute things. I was actively and finally enjoying studying for the first time in a while since changing my major. I was in the study room, sitting near the windows that surrounded me in the front and on the left side, and there were two girls and a guy on the other side of the room, studying for another test. In the middle of studying, I just happened to look up and there was this guy walking past the window. I had seen him maybe once in another building but never before. Which was weird because being at a PWI (predominately white institution), all the black people for the most part, know each other or know of one another. From either in class, at a kickback, at a party, working on campus, or in an organization. But this guy, I felt like I

hadn't seen him before, anywhere. I literally remember thinking when I walked past him for the first time, "Man it's like that guy dropped from the sky, I've never seen him before". My exact words.

Since I had seen him once before, I smiled and he smiled back then waved. Then I just went back to studying. Didn't really think much of it, like I said…for once I was actually studying. Since my class was canceled, I just stayed through the normal class session in the study area to finish studying. Then the classes let out of that session and the next session was about to start and I started reviewing the last few sentences of my notes because I needed to start packing up soon to go take my test. Then I look up again and there goes the guy walking past again, I smile again but this time he makes his way to the door of the study room. My stomach kinda did this flip thing and I was like "umm alright stomach, I'm going to need you to get it all the way

together" Like who gives their stomach a pep talk? Yep, me. He opens the door, and says, "Hi, my name is Glenn. What's yours?"

I smile and respond, "Bianca."

"Nice to meet you Bianca, I know this is kind of forward but could I have your number?"

Now mind you the other people studying…yup still there. I don't think he noticed them but I kept feeling like wow this is sweet and embarrassing all at the same time! I usually would brush guys off because of the season I was in, trying to focus on me and graduating, but something felt different about him. I

felt a genuineness and kindness about him, I never really felt before when I met other guys for the first time. So, I did it. "Sure." He pulled out his blackberry phone, yes I said blackberry in 2014, he denies this to this day but I'll never forget that, I thought it was too funny. He said he'll text me and walked away back down the hallway. Now my smiley self looking down at my notes, trying to retain the sentence I read about three times over and over, at the same time

thinking "okay that just happened" then I finally was like "Bianca. You might as well pack up and go to class because you're not about to concentrate after that."

Laughing at myself, I started packing up my stuff and one of the voices from the other side of the room spoke up, "Hey, have you met him before?" I just realized I knew the guy studying, he was a friend from one of my classes, and I laughed walking out the door, "Nope, I haven't. Crazy right?"

After a couple weeks of getting to know one another which was full of texting, phone calls, instant messaging, snapchats, meetups for lunch, walks to and from class….I was like you know, I think I might kinda like this guy. We talked about any and everything. I loved it. I felt like I could literally talk to him about anything. He is a dreamer and realist all in one and he was a Christian too. He led a small group with a Christian organization and everything right there at school! I've truly never met anyone like him before.

By this point, we started getting into tougher conversations, and here came the famous one for me….waiting for marriage. I was like okay, let me see what he was going to say. Usually at this point talking to a guy, I'm always the

first one to say exactly how I feel and why I'm waiting with sternness to the point where I'm almost being dismissive or just giving them an out. Letting them know that I am waiting for sex and no, I will not change my mind whatever you try and do. I think a part of me was making sure it was known in the beginning so I wasn't leading anyone on but I think now, there was also a

part of me that said it to put a wall up to protect me emotionally to see who would take the time to knock down the wall brick by brick to really get to know me. The real me, not what I allowed you to see. But this time, for the first time, was different. He told ME how he felt, and he said it first.

"So, I know this might sound crazy and I hope this doesn't turn you off from wanting to continue to get to know me because I do want to continue this with you." Now I'm all invested at this point because I'm like okay he's about to tell me he just got out of jail or has four babies by four different mothers back at home, my mind just went all left with him saying that one sentence.

"So, I'm celibate. I've been celibate for 5 years since committing my life to Christ, and I plan on waiting to have sex again with the woman I marry, on our wedding night." At this moment, picture my mouth dropping all the way onto the floor like a cartoon, eyes wide open, hand waving in the air like wait… wait…wait a got dang minute! Yeah, I said it! Wait, A guy in college. Over 18 years old. Had previous relationships that were sexual but is still waiting for

marriage?! LIKE WHAT?! God, you are a whole comedian, because I know this can only be from You! It has got to be!! From what everyone said around me for the last few years that would never happen but here is this guy standing right in front of me defying everything they said. Only God. But I'm not going to jump there in my head like I did last time. I'm just going to keep talking and tell him my stance. "Wow that's so crazy you said that because I'm a virgin and

I'm waiting for marriage too." He looked at me with the same crazy face as I did.

**I Do!**

Fast forward two and a half years. I'm in my wedding dress that couldn't have been more perfect for me. Just the perfect mix of lace, pearls, and sparkle with a veil that stretched down the aisle to match. I looked in the mirror like wow, this really is happening. I really prayed for this guy and God supplied him, just as simple as that. I trusted that God would answer my prayer and

bring me the guy that surpassed everything I could have asked for. Not just him, but his mother who is truly a second mother to me, I gained a sister who truly became my sister, and two brothers, grandmother, aunt, uncles, truly a family who embraced me. Nobody could have done what was done here. Nobody. Only Jesus. It was time. I pick up my dress, with the help of some of my closest girls and start walking towards the doors of the church. I grab my dad's arm, who's smiling from ear to ear. I hear the song, and at that moment Whitney's words sent chills up my spine. I start walking to her words, stepping with confirmation in every word she says. "I Believe in you and me. I believe that we will be in love eternally, well as far as I can see, you will always be the one for me. Oh yes you will…." I heard the sniffs in the audience, and I felt it too…the power in that moment, what it really meant for me walking up to the altar, my dad giving Glenn my hand, and us walking up to exchange vows, I get it. One of the biggest moments of my life. "Bianca, it feels like yesterday."

Before today I had never seen Glenn cry. I think it was hitting him too, the commitment we were making. It was beautiful and powerful all at the same time. Now we couldn't have imagined how long Glenn would be crying, by this time bawling…loudly, to the point where it took his brother to come up onto stage to calm him down and now my poor husband is the butt of every joke with his close friends when it comes to crying at weddings. "Well, I cried but it wasn't Glenn level crying!" It's funny, but honestly, it was just showing yet again another one of the attributes that initially attracted me to him, his genuineness. He's not a man's man trying to prove every second that he's a "tough guy," he's exactly who God knew I needed. Someone who was secure in himself being God's child and loving me for me in the way that only God can show him how. Completely and passionately.

"Bianca, it feels like only yesterday we started dating and now we are getting married. God was really looking out for me when I met you. We are a match made in heaven. Bianca, you are a special woman whom I promise to cherish and love from this day on. Bianca, you are my angel. I heard it said, 'I see these vows not as promises but as privileges: I get to laugh with you, cry with you, care for you, share with you, I get to run with you, walk with you, build with you, live with you!' I do solemnly resolve before God to take full responsibility for myself, my wife, and my future children. I will courageously work with the strength God provides to fulfill these vows for the rest of my life and for His glory." ......whew when I say there wasn't a dry eye in the room!

My babe always has a way with words. "Glenn, today in front of my most cherished loved ones, I choose you. I choose to follow you, respect you, and always love you. I promise to support you, be your partner, your advisor, and biggest fan. I promise to always strive to be the best wife God calls me to be for you. I promise to always be your cuddle bug and cupcake, just keep being my superman. I can't promise you dark days will never come but I can promise to always be your safe place, to listen, and always be here for you to lift you up when you're down. I am so thankful that God allowed our paths to cross, because by meeting you, loving you, and now becoming your wife, my faith has become even stronger because it's showed me once again that God answers prayers. No measure of time with you is long enough but let's start with forever."

and just like that, husband and wife. That day was indescribable.

Definitely, on the books as one of my favorite days ever thus far. It was filled with so much love to the point where you can say God had to be in the room. Great food, great music, and most of all, loved ones from all over the country. Glenn was born in Philly and most of his family that were there he hadn't seen in almost 10 years. They came down in support of him because of the man he is.

**Warning: Reaching Married People conversations**

As we "sparkled" our way to Glenn's car, driving away from the church to our hotel. We just kept looking at each other, in his tux, in my gown…like wow we really just got married! I think we even laughed about it at one point. We got to the hotel, exhausted but still awake because of what the rest of the night entails. I changed into my wedding night lingerie, which was so

beautiful, white and lacy, I was so excited to wear…I mean c'mon I waited what seemed like forever for this night! And it was beautiful. I enjoyed the foreplay, because being real…we knew how to foreplay, it was the rest that was approaching new territory for us. And the rest…. HURT. Laying there, my face started to cringe. Is it supposed to hurt this bad? Glenn noticed my face

and stopped immediately.

"What's wrong?? Are you okay" he asked.

"It just hurts more than I thought it would" I said softly.

"Do you want me to stop??" As he's already getting off of me.

"No, It's okay. My body will get used to it, I'm sure."

It didn't, it still hurt, but I just tried not to show it, so it would be a good experience for him. I remember laying there, after and Glenn was in heaven almost and don't get me wrong I enjoyed myself, but I couldn't help but think…will it always be like this? Will sex always hurt for me? I also was afraid to mention to Glenn…I eventually did but I right afterwards… I actually felt dirty, like I committed a sin. I realized at that moment and the days after I realized how much I really didn't know about sex and what sex looked like within a healthy marriage. Also, my parents, church family, family, married friends, etc. who always preached about abstinence and waiting for marriage never gave me guidance on what happens next. How to flip that "sexual sin switch" from single, virgin to being married and sexually active.

My whole life was "Don't have sex. Abstain from sex. Sex is bad. Sex is dirty. You'll feel dirty, be dirty. Sex is sinful. Sex will get you pregnant. Sex will give you STDs. Sex will get your feelings hurt, heartbroken." Years and years of hearing these statements, thinking these thoughts and honestly, as I got older, I would fuel these thoughts as motivation. It became a sort of defense mechanism for when it got harder to ignore what my body was naturally craving. It would work because I didn't want to be "dirty" or sinful. I wanted to please God and not sin, so there we go I won't have sex. But what happens when you tell yourself these thoughts (truth or not) for over 15 years? It stays with you, lingering in the subconscious. I thought my struggle was something I only dealt with until I talked with another friend who also waited until marriage to have sex and she said she went through a similar experience. She felt dirty and ashamed after making love to her husband. It's so crazy to me because, as Christians, we never talk about this.

We never talk about what it feels like to tell yourself for over 15 years that sex is sinful and "dirty" but have to flip that switch in one night, no matter how special it is. Plus, after having waited this long to have sex, especially with someone I truly loved…I mean in the movies they're not dirty. They have rose petals leading up to the bed, they have sex on the counter, in the car, in the shower and she's glowing and smiling…I mean they are always ready, and they seem like they're having a great time! So, why do I feel like this? Why can't I shake this "Sex equals sin" out of my head?!

The first year, sexually, was tough for our marriage. Mostly because of me, being honest. I loved my husband and was physically attracted to him, I just never wanted to have sex. It seemed like every time it would hurt, and I felt like I just sinned afterwards. I just didn't want to feel like that anymore, so I would give any reason I could possibly think of not to have sex. I knew that God wanted me to wait until marriage, I knew that sex was created in the confines of marriage. I totally understand and can see that because sex is actually quite beautiful, but it has to be with the right person. But I just couldn't get my mind there for the first year or two after our marriage.

**The Talk**

"Sex is for marriage. Period. Don't let boys go anywhere near you down there because that's all they want." Love my parents, but that pretty much summed up my sex talk. Now, don't get me wrong, I was happy it wasn't longer than that, because teenage-me wasn't ready to have a longer conversation with my parents because I mean, awkward. But I also think they were concerned about saying the right thing and not the wrong thing. Which to their defense, it's a pretty tough conversation coming from a parent's perspective. However, looking back, and to where I am now, I think I needed help understanding my body without judgment or consequence. I think my mom tried to have my gynecologist do that for me, but my doctor came from a "doctor perspective" and my mom also refused, as my advocate, to leave the room during our appointments so there's only so many questions I'm going to ask in front my mom, being honest.

Also, once I asked more questions once I got married, my doctor would answer them but kind of in a way that assumed I should already know the answer. Which to her defense, by this age, I probably should have. I didn't really know what my body make up was like, where everything was, what everything was named, what happened to my body during sex, how sex affects your hormone imbalance. A lot of things. Glenn and I can communicate about anything, but this was different. How am I going to communicate what's going on with me when I don't even know what's going on to even communicate it to him?! There were so many layers of things I just truly didn't understand about myself. Intimacy physically, emotionally, all of it. Even down to receiving affection from Glenn.

**The Work**

I realized how much work had to be done, needed to be done. First, I needed to remember that God made my body, and He is the source of what I needed and had the answers to all the questions I had. By seeking Him first. Second, I had to realize that Glenn is my partner, my teammate. I needed to tell him what I'm going through and what I had been feeling, just being honest then trusting vulnerability with my partner. After we talked, Glenn suggested we pray about it together and after 6 years, we are still praying and seeing the rewards of those prayers. It's been a journey but who says it was supposed to be easy? But what can I say?

God prepared me in my journey of abstinence. I learned how to be patient and it allowed me to take my time and learn how to enjoy my sexuality with my husband. Glenn also prepared himself through his celibacy journey before we even stepped on that altar to say, "I do". Not saying that it didn't get tough for him, but he didn't get impatient and step outside of our marriage like others without that preparation might have done. We had to trust.

I trusted God to be that same God that I prayed to, sitting in my college apartment on Valentine's Day. When my friends and I did a group date with our boyfriends and after the night was done my friends went off to their rooms with their boyfriends doing married people things and Glenn said it was too much temptation for us to just hang out tonight, so we'll have to call it a night and that he'll call me in the morning. In that moment, I thanked God for bringing someone who would hold me accountable, but I trusted that one day we'll be able to do married people's things, on Valentine's Day, as a married couple. I also must continuously and genuinely close the door to what I think I want, so God can open the door to what I need. I mean look at the simple fact when Glenn came into my life. God had to close the door to my ex that Thursday, so God could open the door to my husband and three beautiful kids on Monday!

Ladies, you have to genuinely trust God when you wait and put aside what you think you want so God can show you what you need. The same God that got me here was the same faithful God that brought me my husband despite what people said. He was that same God! I knew that same God could totally change my perspective on sex/making love, and He did. He was the only one that could have. Not me, not Glenn, not my parents, not my doctor, no one…only God. After staying in the word of God, staying in prayer with my husband over our love life, God rewarded and blessed our journey because we were faithful then and we were faithful now. I needed Him to show me my partner who was literally right in front of me. To show me how to communicate to Glenn what was going on inside my head. We ended up just giving our bedroom over to God and that allowed me to see that being intimate with my husband is a beautiful expression of love and is fun! Yes, nothing is perfect, it will hurt at first, physically, but it will hurt less and less until it doesn't anymore. I mean in 5 years we had 3 kids, so God allowed us to figure it out for sure!

All roads lead to and from God and He is and will always be faithful. Just rest in that ladies and gents, don't lose faith in the journey. Just stay the course and He will honor that. I'm a living witness. I'm just grateful He chose me to complete my assignment of being faithful in my journey of abstinence.

"…You will always harvest what you plant. Those who live only to satisfy their own sinful nature will harvest decay and death from that sinful nature. But those who live to please the Spirit will harvest everlasting life from the Spirit. So, let's not get tired of doing what is good. At just the right time we will reap a harvest of blessing if we don't give up." – Galatians 6: 7-9

**The Pretty  on the Outside, Hurting on the Inside,**
**But God Gave Me a Do Over~ KnaKita Jones**

It's ironic that my friend asked me to contribute to this book concerning "assignment" and "purpose" around the same time that I finally began a deep dive into who I am.

Honestly, I started to process my life's experiences differently as I matured. I had recently found myself hurting emotionally, in pain physically and disappointment thoroughly, but this time it was different feelings and I knew I would be better after going through the healing process this time! I began to understand that oftentimes growing, healing and recovering is painful.

For years, even as a believer in Christ, I didn't understand why I was experiencing so much hurt and pain throughout my life. I finally realized that God was doing his part my entire life and I was missing his plan and purpose for me. God was always there, the answers to my questions were in plain sight, but I had continued to miss the simple answer for years.

What was the lesson that God has been teaching me? What have I been missing? How has my disobedience impacted me, my children, my grandchildren, my loved ones and others?  Who am I supposed to help in this life, what is my greater purpose? I pray that sharing some of the personal and unflattering details about my life helps others heal, release some hurt and pain, and help some own and release the lies they've been living with, as well.

Throughout my years I've heard people talk about relationships with their parents, siblings, aunts, uncles, spouses and others. Some admit that many of those relationships are not what they appeared to be. The healthy relationship struggle is real and we have to start facing some hard realities and make some changes in ourselves in order to learn, to grow. My chapter in this book is not intended to hurt, shame or disrespect anyone, it's what I need to share and release to continue my healing process. It may not be popular, but it's my truth. I sincerely hope it helps others find and own their truth as well.

I am 63 years young (at the time of this writing) and I am truly "grateful and blessed" at this point in my life. I've said that many times before but I didn't really feel it. I thought it was just the right thing to say at the time. I've never been much of a complainer. Even when in pain I've dealt with most issues without the help of others.  God was always there, but I didn't always call on him. I must admit that I have many "shoulda," "coulda" and "wouldas" in my life. Unfortunately, God doesn't give us a dress rehearsal for life. This is it; there are no do-overs.  We can and should learn from our mistakes and do things differently the next time. But let's face it, a mistake, a lie, a bad choice, a sin, it is what it is, and it can't be undone, but it can be forgiven.

We are molded from childhood and things we see, hear, experience affect us tremendously, sometimes for the good, but many times for bad. God wants to give us peace before, after and even during the storms of life, he's always there, but we don't always trust that his way is the better way.

I want to share a little about who I am, where I came from and how my dysfunction began many years ago and some of you will be able to relate. I don't want sympathy for anything that I've experienced as an adult. I made choices, and good or bad I'm now able to own them.

I was a pretty baby. I was a pretty little girl. I was a beautiful teenager, a beautiful adult and I'm an attractive woman now as a senior. At this point, my age is starting to show with gray hair, some extra undesired pounds and moving slower too, but still attractive by many standards.

As a little girl, men and women would often say how pretty I was. Men, young and old, would say "you're going to be a heartbreaker." I heard it from young guys, but most often from guys who were older and should not have been making these types of comments to a young girl. I guess it was supposed to be a compliment, but as I think back, I realize it was inappropriate flirtation.

I've always known that I was attractive, and in many ways different too. As a younger woman I never took compliments well, I would usually play them down, but now I'm finally able to receive a compliment with grace and own it.

I also remember hearing that "pretty is, as pretty does," so I've tried to be a team player even to the point of allowing the other team to win, in different areas of my life.

Both of my parents were born and raised in a small town called Minden, Louisiana in the late 1930s. Dad was an only child, he was handsome, his parents were able to provide for him very well and he was popular too. I had the privilege and honor of knowing my paternal grandparents. My grandfather (Daddy Walter) was a kind, gentle, soft spoken, hardworking man that owned land, horses and cows in the country and didn't talk much, but loved deeply. My grandmother (Mama Rixie) was much more outspoken and could and would curse with the best of them. She loved to laugh.. She was smart, and as a young woman she owned a beauty salon and a beauty school too. During that era Black folks had to own their own due to segregation during the Jim Crow era.

I remember her helping many people in our small town, she had a big heart and was always giving and not expecting anything in return. My brother and I were both the apples of her eyes and she very seldom said no to us about anything. Unfortunately, my grandparents grew apart and divorced. It is my belief that their divorce largely contributed to my dad's sense of brokenness.

My mom had a much more modest background. She and her younger brother Gerald lost their mother Lucille to tuberculosis when mom was 4 years old and my uncle was 2 years old. A few years later they lost their father Roderick to heart disease when they were 12 and 10 years old. I can't imagine the type of loss and childhood pain they experienced so young. Oh but, they had a loving, kind and praying grandmother (Mama Mallie) and even though she didn't have much, what she had was theirs too!

I had the privilege of knowing her and she was beautiful, with long wavy hair, kind, soft spoken, a truth teller and she was the one person that I can say prayed every night. She would kneel on her knees, next to her bed so often that she had knee prints on the floor. I saw for myself and heard from countless others that she was one of the best seamstresses of her time. My mom said she and her brother didn't realize that they were different from other kids that grew up with both parents, because their grandmother loved them just as if she birthed them herself. Still today, I believe she was the sweetest, kindest, most unselfish person I have ever known.

My mom and dad grew up and went to school together all their lives, fell in love, and married in our small town. They were young when they married, young when they had my brother, then two years later still young when I was born. My parents gave my brother and I most of the material things we asked for as kids and they stayed married until we were grown. I had a good childhood, but what I didn't know then was that their unhealthy marriage would affect me and my decision making for years to come.

I have many fun and happy memories as a kid. I remember so many great holiday gatherings, birthday parties, drive-in movies, trips to the lake and vacations that we shared as a family. We didn't travel a lot, but two vacations I vividly remember with much joy were our trip to Galveston Beach and a train ride we took to Kansas City. Great memories.

My parents made sure we stayed active, my brother in sports and band, and I in dance, cheer, modeling, pageants, majorette, drill team, etc. That's what I meant when I said earlier, we had a good childhood.  Dad treated me like his princess as a little girl, but unfortunately, many times he didn't treat mom like the queen he should have, as his wife. I mentioned earlier that my dad was broken and suffered from unhealed hurt. And his brokenness was amplified by alcohol. The alcohol made him angry and one way the anger came out was sometimes mistreating mom. They shared good times, as well. They would sometimes go out to one of the Black-owned clubs or little holes in the wall in Minden. I remember my parents going away together a few times, and my brother and I would stay with one of my grandparents and that was always a treat.

Hardys Kindergarten was the only Black kindergarten in town and was a staple in our community for many years. I have a lot of good memories about that place. My elementary school teachers were tough, no nonsense, but loving, kind and caring too. I loved and admired all of them, but there was one teacher that stood out most for me, and her name was Mrs. Amos. She was extra kind, caring and patient. She died many years ago, but every time I think of her, I smile.

Minden was considered safe for children to play outside, so we walked to the swimming pool and stayed for hours. As we got older, we were allowed to go to Joe's Dixie Cream for some of the best hamburgers, french fries, milkshakes and ice cream cones on this side of heaven. Later, they built a recreation center (The Rec), and it became a hangout and a safe place for children, teenagers and young adults, as well.

There was a popular corner in Minden that I visited almost every day with my dad, because it had several Black-owned businesses that he would frequent. There was Jack Jones Filling Station, Mrs. Worthy's Store, Brek's Place, Jewel Martins Auto Shop and others too. Good memories, good times and good people, as well. There are many successful people that came from Minden; athletics, entertainers, politicians etc. and their names are known throughout the world.

There was a lot of good that happened in Minden and there was life happening as well, and it was not hard to hear rumors and scandals in the town too. This isn't new or isolated to my hometown; sin is worldwide and it affects individuals and whole families too. I'm just sharing some of my experiences as a child in my hometown and how some of the things I heard, saw and experienced affected me.

As kids, some of my friends and I heard rumors of married people having affairs or having children with people other than their spouses, men having two families, single people dating married people, etc. We heard about kids being raised as cousins though they were actually siblings. Many of the people I heard rumors about were people that I admired and respected and I wondered what was true and what wasn't. As kids we would talk amongst ourselves, but most times we wouldn't ask for clarification because unlike today, kids were expected to be seen and not heard. As many of us know, back then, children didn't get into grown folk's business and there were consequences if we tried. Thinking back now, we should have been able to talk to our parents about anything that we didn't understand. When we hold things in, hiding, pretending an injustice didn't happen when it actually did, it usually causes more pain and many times scared kids turn into scared adults.

We heard all sorts of things and didn't realize it at the time, but it would affect many of us negatively as we became adults, had relationships, got married and started our own families. I can speak for myself; many things from my childhood created negative thoughts, and sometimes those thoughts become actions and some of those actions would not serve me well.

My parents would argue, fuss and fight when I was a kid and the root of many of those arguments was because my dad was seeing other women. Minden has grown over the years, but 60 years ago it was smaller and everyone knew everyone, and sometimes family business didn't stay in the house. If a spouse was cheating the odds were very good that the other spouse knew the other woman or man. Total disrespect. It took me a long time to even acknowledge the women that were involved in the cheating rumors with my dad. I was even told as a child that my dad had another daughter, which meant I had a sister, but until this day it's unconfirmed, so we grew up not knowing for sure.

At some point, we must heal, forgive, let it go and move on, right? However, I deceived myself for years. I thought, "Out of sight, out of mind." But what I thought was healed has shown up in my life on rotation, throughout my life. And I am not alone; there are many adults dealing with unhealed hurt and pain and they are going through life smiling while hurting on the inside. Some adults admit that they experienced physical, mental, emotional trauma and unfortunately some dealt with sexual abuse in their childhoods too. I now understand if we don't own our issues, it's hard to heal from what we don't acknowledge.

When I was a child, most people didn't talk about abuse, trauma, brokenness, hurt and pain. They were too ashamed to admit it, so most tried to hide the dysfunction in the family more often than not. What we didn't know back then is all families were dealing with some sort of dysfunction. It may not have been what your family was dealing with, but if they were to open their closets, the skeletons would fall out.

I experienced an incident of sexual abuse as a child and none of my family and friends knew. One of my dad's friends/acquaintances touched me inappropriately as a little girl. I kept my distance from him after that, but I never told anyone. I carried shame, disappointment and an unanswered question of "why," for many years. Why would a grown man touch a little girl in a sexual way? It made no sense then and it makes no sense today. I didn't tell my mom, because she would've told my dad and I knew his temper would cause him to do something that may send him to jail, and I didn't want that. Much later, as an adult, I was raped at knife point, by a man I didn't know. I begged him out loud not to kill me, while praying silently and by the grace of God, my life was spared. I put those hurts, pains and injustices out of my conscious mind, but I didn't realize that the subconscious mind was much more powerful. Many men and women have experienced sexual abuse, but never talk about it or even acknowledge that it happened.

I was sprinkled at the altar at Mount Zion C.M.E. Church as a child which meant I was dedicated back to the Lord. My mom told me about it, and I believe even with all of the turmoil throughout my life, dedicating me back to the Lord at a young age has been my "saving grace".

I stopped regularly attending church for a few years as a young adult, but I still wanted to please God with my life. It goes without saying, but I'll say it anyway, I missed the mark, repeatedly. As a young adult, I thought I was a Christian because I went to church sometimes, I read the bible sometimes, I prayed sometimes, I was a nice person most of the time. And when I did slip up, I would ask for forgiveness, when I committed sin, I would repent. That's what a Christian did right; they'd sin and repent? When I found the scripture where Paul said in the Bible *"Oh ratcheted man I am and even when I want to do good, I find myself doing bad, "* that was confirmation that I was okay. Even Paul couldn't get it right.

If I could have some "do overs" life would be very different. I didn't know the importance of true repentance, I wasn't a Christian, I had deceived myself for years and I was playing church. I'm so grateful to the Lord that I didn't die during those years, because I would have gone to Hell.

A few years later, I found my way back to church, accepted Jesus Christ as my Lord and savior, truly believed that he died for my sins, confessed it, was baptized and continued to grow in the word and the things of God. The enemy's job is to kill, steal and destroy. He's good at what he does, and he's continuing to destroy lives today. Even with all the attacks on my life and my own bad decisions/choices, I'm still standing because the Lord has work for me to do. Like many others, even after accepting Christ, I continued to make bad choices and decisions which you will read about here. Two words: mercy and grace.

I had my heart set on meeting and marrying the love of my life that God chose and staying married until one of us died. I was determined to be different from my mom. I wasn't going to tolerate the things she tolerated, and I was going to have a better marriage than my parents and many others that I saw. My determination not to tolerate certain things may have gone to the extreme. As you read on, you will see what I thought would be my reality, would not. I had no idea of the heartache and pain I would experience over the next 40 years of my life.

My family moved from Minden to Dallas when I was in middle school. I enjoyed my middle school and high school years in Dallas and things were better between my parents too. I got good grades; I was on the student council and the Drill Team, and I was popular. I graduated high school at 17 and went to North Texas State University the following year.

From the time I was a little girl and throughout high school, I wanted to be a news commentator. I used to watch Barbara Walters with my great-grandmother, Mama Mallie, every evening and I wanted to be on the TV news just like her. If I had only continued to pursue that dream… I was smart, attractive, articulate, personable and I would have made an amazing news commentator. The worst kind of letdown is when you do it to yourself. I didn't know my value. I started playing small at a young age to keep others comfortable. This would affect my relationships, romantic and otherwise, and years later it would also affect my relationship with my children.

I declared a major in journalism/communication and I was on my way to being a news commentator; or so I thought. Externally, it appeared that I was good, I was pretty, smart, thin, long hair, but internally I was a mess. I started to look for love in all the wrong places and within two weeks of being on campus, I met an attractive, tall, dark and handsome football player and we allowed ourselves to get distracted with each other during our freshman year in college.

We dated the first semester and by the second semester my boyfriend decided to transfer from NTSU to TSU to play football the following year. Over the summer, I finally got my nerve up to ask my dad (strict dad) if I could transfer, and much to my surprise he said "yes." My boyfriend and I were both naïve, somewhat sheltered and all that freedom would soon be a detriment to us both.

We transferred schools, moved to Houston and continued our relationship, and guess what. Not long after, I was 19 and pregnant. I loved my dad, and back then, many parents had the attitude that if you get pregnant before marriage, you get married as soon as possible, as though that would reverse the order of things. So, we got married and neither of us were ready or prepared for the commitment of marriage.

I, for sure, was not prepared to be a wife, a mother, and be a student too. It was overwhelming. Why did I think I could have a husband, have a baby and have good grades too? I was keeping busy so I didn't have to be with myself. I still didn't recognize or own that I was carrying unresolved, unidentified hurt, pain, disappointment and even resentment. I continued to cover up all the negatives with nice clothes, a great personality and a smile. I wonder how life would have been different if I had recognized my dysfunction and started to work on healing sooner.

My new husband didn't realize it at the time, but he had also experienced childhood trauma from the death of his mother at a young age. Oftentimes, people don't realize how childhood experiences affect them until much later in life, and even then, many don't address it. Most parents do the best they know how when raising children, and unfortunately many times it doesn't turn out as planned.

My husband and I were young, ill-prepared and we struggled in every area: financially, emotionally and spiritually. And we argued a lot. When I was young, I was small, but I would not back down from a fight. Remember, I was determined to be different from my mom. I've never been a person to use foul language. It has always vexed my spirit and it still does today. I would not curse him during an argument, but I would say hurtful things that did not serve the marriage well. We did not honor the part of the marriage vows that said "until death do us part," and I found myself divorced at 22 years old. If I could have a "do over."

I stayed in Houston after the divorce. I was still in school, working, raising my son and we were good. A few years later I met a man, we dated for a couple of years and then we married. We both had sons about the same age, we bought a house and life was good, for a little while. Early in the marriage there was deception on both sides which caused trust to be questioned, and that can be a recipe for disaster. I am here to own my part and I deceived my husband by omission, in not sharing my intent to have another baby. Big mistake.

He wasn't sure if he wanted more children at this point, but I did, so I stopped taking the pill and shortly after, I was pregnant. I wanted a little girl and I wanted her by age 30. She was born one day before my 30th birthday. You've probably heard the saying "What's done in the dark, will come to light." The question is not "if," it's "when." Shortly after our daughter was born God allowed my deception to be revealed to my husband. I was wrong and there is nothing I can say to make it right. I was selfish. The marriage survived for a while, but it started to break down and divorce soon followed. I brought my pain into the marriage and once again, I married a man who had his own pain too. He was dealing with losing his mom at an early age. We were two hurting people unwilling to fight for the commitment of marriage.

I was single again; now with two children. My situation was not ideal, but I was okay, or so I thought. I still didn't see the need for counseling or to surrender everything to the Lord. If only I could have a do-over.

I was not actively looking for a relationship, but I still had a desire to be married and I was determined to have a good and successful marriage one day. By now you see it was not hard for me to meet men or to get married. I was pretty, I had a nice personality, I worked and I loved God, so I attracted men. After a while, I met a man who was kind, funny, had a nice car, and had a good job, all pluses for me at the time. We dated for several months and soon he loved me and wanted to make a family with me and my children, so we married and we were together for 17 years!

Later we had a daughter, as well. The marriage was good for many years, but again I attracted a man that had unresolved pain and he masked his pain with alcohol. I still wasn't the whole, healed woman I should have been either. I truly wish I had known then, what I know today, I would have loved him differently. We both allowed the breakdown of the marriage and it ended in divorce. If I could have a do-over.

Unfortunately, it has taken the majority of my life to recognize and own my hurt, start to deal with it and realize that healing from life is not an option, it's a requirement, for me, my children and my grandchildren.

As I look back today, each of my husbands had at least one character trait of my dad, including, but not limited to some type of childhood dysfunction/trauma. This is not to say that all adults are hurting from their childhood, but many are. I hear people say "Let the past stay in the past," "Let sleeping dogs lie." But unless the trauma is dealt with, it doesn't go away, it's just hidden under the surface. Some people identify their pain early and get the help they need and are able to have loving, caring, faithful relationships and marriages, so it's not an absolute that seeing bad or broken marriages will cause you to have one, generally speaking.

My parents' marriage ended in divorce, and as mentioned earlier my grandparents divorced too. It's not an excuse, it's just a fact; I didn't have many solid/happy marriages to admire and/or emulate in my family. My parents and grandparents were good people, but broken for one reason or another and they didn't identify what it was and how to fix it. I had the privilege and the honor of knowing two of my great-grandmothers before they passed, and they were both single. When my paternal grandparents divorced from each other, they never remarried. We have a small family and to this day I can only think of my mother's brother and his wife as a great example of marriage. I was in their wedding and 60 years later, they are still married and in love. This was the only happy marriage in my immediate family that I remember from childhood. I've had conversations with my uncle as an adult, and the love and admiration he has for his wife is genuine and it shows. Thanks Uncle Gerald and Aunt Pat.

I have friends now in their 50s & 60s that's had the desire to be married for years, but for one reason or another, they have not made it to the altar. They experienced "love" and had children, but never married. One of them is a co-author of this book and we both have three children by three different men although our paths were quite different. I have other friends that are married and unhappy, but they stay and go to bed many nights asking "What if"? I know people that stay in the marriage but have affairs and are convinced that it's better than divorce. Is it or is it not?

I also have friends that are in happy marriages, but unfortunately that list is the shortest. I celebrate my friends that are happy in marriage because in that area of life they pleased the Lord, because marriage is important to God. Marriage takes work, so for those that are doing it well, congratulations. I've had more than my share of marriages and I know that was not God's plan for my life and as you've read throughout this story, it wasn't my plan either.

40

I am not giving myself a pass. I wanted it to be easier and I gave up when things got hard. I have conversations with God about love, relationships and marriages. "Why do so many good people have bad marriages and why so many divorces? How can we heal and stop the pain of broken relations for ourselves, our children and our children's children?" His answer: talk about it.

For those of you that married as virgins, have only known one sexual partner in your lifetime and survived the hard times, great job! You followed God's blueprint and I pray that the Lord will continue to bless and keep you, your spouse and your marriage until death separates you. For everyone else, please know that God loves you, he can still use you, he has a plan and purpose for your life, as well, and forgiveness is possible with true repentance. God doesn't stop loving us even in disobedience, even though there are consequences. There is healing power in the name of Jesus and if we desire to heal and get better, we can. It's going to take work; acknowledge that hurt and pain exist, identify the source of the pain and then start the healing, purging and redemption process.

Many people reading this have experienced divorce at some point and maybe even recently. If that's you, just know there can be joy on the other side, don't give up, don't allow bitterness and anger to consume you. Keep getting up, keep living, you'll be okay, and remember, it's darkest right before the day breaks. Don't ever allow those that haven't gone through the pain of divorce make you feel unworthy of God's love. That may not be their sin, but they have others! It's unfortunate that many times people condemn others for their public sin and many of them are doing ungodly things, in the dark. Just know that God does not sleep and all of our sins will be revealed sooner or later because acknowledging the sin is a part of the healing process.

I won't give this much space, but I must mention it because it's a significant part of my healing and realization that I'm stronger than I thought. I met a man a few years ago and I didn't follow my first thought, not to get to know him. Big mistake. We were both older, attending church, he was teaching Bible study and Sunday school, we both had previous relationships that ended in hurt. I thought we were both ready to live our latter years loving God, each other, our children and grandchildren, but I could not have been more WRONG.

The treatment that I received in that relationship was worse than anything I had ever experienced in my entire life, by anyone. The lies, the adultery, the deceit, the pretense and the blatant disrespect was crushing. He was dealing with a lot of dysfunction, hurt, pain and abandonment issues.

When all of his secrets and lies started to be revealed and after I accepted that I didn't know him as well as I thought, it was easier to walk away. When I did, I felt free, peace, joy and a heavy burden lifted. It wasn't immediate, but a few months after I left, I knew I was truly on a path of healing from him and of my past. It was difficult, but when I started to pray for him (and the woman he cheated with), instead of being angry whenever they came to mind, I knew I had forgiven them both. When you can truly ask the Lord to forgive and bless those that hurt you, you are on the road to recovery and God is pleased.

I believe that God allowed me to experience heartache, pain and disappointment for much of my life because he loves me so much he let me make the choices that brought about the negative experiences. I'm grateful that he didn't give up on me. He knew all along, I was one of his prodigal daughters. I was self-dependent, not God-dependent and I was also looking for a man to fill a space that was shaped especially and only for God. I thank God for Jesus, his love, his mercy and grace.

Most of my adult life I was pouring from a half empty, sometimes totally empty cup and the old saying is true, "Nothing from nothing, leaves nothing." I was growing older but wasn't getting better because I had not acknowledged, admitted or identified my brokenness. Even though I've not experienced a lifelong love and the successful marriage that I desired, I've learned a lot. I'm a better person today than ever before and life is good. I'm purposely single and loving it.

I was so undeserving of a do-over and another do-over and another do-over, but God loved me so much that he didn't allow me to graduate until I learned the lesson. I've been a believer and follower of Christ for many years, but the simple lesson alluded me until very recently. I can finally say, "I got it." God was then, God is now, and God will always be enough. I was trying to make a man my source, when the man was only meant to be a resource; God was always my source. I am totally looking at the woman in the mirror and I own my part in the demise of my marriages, and I will leave the rest to the Lord.

Many types of relationships are suffering in today's world, not just romantic ones. Parents and children, siblings, coworkers, church members and each of us have to ask ourselves, "What's my role in the breakdown of these relationships?" I think if we can get marriages right, we would start to restore and heal our society. When we have two happy, whole, joy-filled adults marrying and becoming parents, we have a better chance of having happy, whole, joy-filled children and much of the dysfunction in the world would flee. It's not a be-all, fix-all, but it's a start.

When the family is good, the churches will be better, the schools will be better, workplaces will be better. There is a rippling effect. When the enemy destroys marriages he has a much easier path to our children, and there lies many of the issues. Marriages are failing in the church as much as they are in the world. We have to truly learn how to love ourselves before we can love others. We have to make time for self-care in every area of our lives and this includes mentally, physically, spiritually, emotionally and financially. There's only one you, no one else can be a better version. The bible says God knew us before he formed us in our mother's womb. How amazing is that? He knew everything about us and he loved us then and he loves us now. In his word, he said, he will never leave us nor forsake us, but we play a part in receiving his goodness.

Men and women have to decide what they have to give and what they want in and from a relationship. Do both of you desire/value the same things and can you openly and honestly discuss those things? Can you trust each other with your secrets, your heart and feel safe? Is God a part of your life and theirs too? We have to be prepared to give each other grace; we all fall short from time to time.

A man said to me recently during a conversation about relationships, and I quote, "Women are too masculine, and they are pushing men away." If this is true, we must ask, why? I don't think the average woman wants to be masculine, but if they are taking on that role, they may feel as though they must invoke that part of the spirit to be effective. Unfortunately, many men are not dependable, faithful, strong, loving, kind, providers, protectors these days. If men are not doing these basic masculine things, some women feel they must do it for themselves and they may become "harder" than they want to be.

I sometimes hear women say, "I don't need a man." In my humble opinion, needing a man doesn't have to be a negative. God created men and women differently, and if we are called by God to be married, we need each other, and that's a good thing. Think about it; if the Lord wanted all of us to be the same, he would have created one gender.

Is there any truth to women being too masculine and men being too feminine? If this is the case, what has happened to cause this gender crisis? It's a battle of the sexes and it was not intended to be. We are supposed to compliment each other. It's not about pointing fingers, it's about figuring out what happened and starting the healing process.

If I'm describing you, try to own it. If it doesn't apply to you, then help a friend who may need it. Women sometimes minimize the fact that men have feelings and needs outside of the physical. Men want to be wanted, respected, needed, loved, listened to, encouraged, supported, complemented, appreciated just like women do. I know it's popular, but I don't totally agree with the phrase "Happy wife, happy life." If once the wife is happy, she gives back and ensures that her husband's desires, wants and needs are met, that's a good thing. If she just assumes that his only desire and purpose in life is to please her while he's suffering in silence, that's not a good marriage and I don't think God is pleased. Generally, women voice their opinions, thoughts and feelings more than men in an intimate relationship. I'm speaking of a relationship absent of physical, mental and/or emotional abuse, if she feels safe, she'll talk.

Men, be the protector of her soul, heart, mind and her body, don't misuse or abuse any part of her.  Love her unconditionally, allow her to exhale and know that you have her back. We should not be competing with each other, most people just want to love and be loved, in spite of our imperfections. The love that Jesus has for us is the model of how we should love each other.

I resented both of my parents for a long time. I resented dad for treating my mom badly and I resented mom for accepting it. As my relationship with God grew, I knew I had to give them grace, because of the grace God had shown me throughout my entire life. I'm grateful to my parents for many things and mostly for loving me and my brother even through their own dysfunction, hurt and pains.

My dad is gone and I'm grateful that he and I were in a good place before he died. I'm even more grateful that we had a conversation months before he got sick, and he told me he had a personal relationship with the Lord, and nothing was better than hearing that. If we have breath in our bodies and we truly believe in our hearts and confess with our mouth that Jesus is Lord and savior, and repent of our sins, we can be saved. In my humble opinion, that's the ultimate. Knowing that our loved ones are with the Lord makes it a little easier to let them go. When we're not sure, that's a hard pill to swallow. Even more important than knowing about your loved ones, is knowing that you have a personal relationship with the Lord and your destiny after leaving here.

Why did I share some of the not so flattering things from my past; where I come from, what I've done and what was done to me? I hope and pray that my past, my story will help others identify and deal with some unhealthy stuff in their lives. I'm sharing from a healing place and I hope and pray that many will start to get better, be better and do better much sooner in life than I did. If this helps one person, it was worth the time, tears and exposure.

I failed miserably at marriage and in other areas, as well. I'm not proud of it and if I had some do-overs I would for sure make different choices. But my past is just that; "my past." You may ask yourself why should I listen to anything she has to say?  You would be correct to ask that question, I've repeatedly made bad choices/decisions and I'm being vulnerable in hopes of helping someone else, and if that's you great. If not; great as well. Seeds are planted. It is easier to learn from other people's mistakes, so you don't have to experience some of the pitfalls for yourself. I asked the Lord to help me share my truth without hurting or embarrassing anyone, especially my children and grandchildren.

I am not a writer, but I know there is a message in my mess. Life is complicated, but good. I can truly say that writing this short story was therapeutic for me. The more I wrote, good and bad thoughts and memories came to mind, but the pain became less and less. I had suppressed many memories for many years, but now I am releasing some of the hurt and pain and I'm ready to live my latter years without drama and regret. I played small for a large part of my life. I've been humble most of my life and many times that was taken as weakness and sometimes I felt like it was. But no more.

I shared things that many of my friends didn't know. I may offend some people because I didn't talk about the Lord enough. I may offend others because I mentioned the Lord too much. That's okay too! I understand that my story is not for everyone, but for those that it's for. I pray that you gain strength from something I've shared.

I won't say that I like everyone from my past, but I will say I'm not angry at anyone, I have no malice or begrudgery in my heart for anyone and God is continuing to purge me of things that don't serve him or myself. I am so far from perfect, but I'm a decent person and I'm growing and getting better every day. I won't ever be perfect on this side of heaven, but I love the Lord, the Lord loves me, and that's enough.

Relationships of all kinds are hard, but they can work if we work at them. We are naturally self-centered, selfish people in need of Jesus. We want our way more often than not, so we usually have to become a person that gives, shares and doesn't demand our way all the time if we are to have a mutually rewarding relationship.

When we are wronged it causes us hurt and pain and many times that produces grudges that we hold on to. There's a saying that "Holding a grudge is like drinking poison and expecting the other person to die." Don't allow the hurt from your past to linger and continue to cause you pain. Try to pray, ask God for help, let it go and heal.

Romans 12:21 says "Do not be overcome by evil, but overcome evil with good." That's not always easy, but it's necessary. There is nothing about my life or yours that surprised God. He knew it would happen before you did. I understand the scripture much better that says *"And we know that all things work together for the good of those that love God and are called according to his purpose."* There were times throughout my life that I've asked, "Why me," but no longer. There's a lot I don't know, but what I do know is, I could not have survived, stayed sane, and be the woman that I am today without the Lord on my side. Love is the key that unlocks the door to forgiveness. So, let's just love more.

**I KNOW WHY THE CAGED MAN CLINGS~ LJ Garfield**

The discussion with my therapist pissed me off again, I understand now why people think therapy is lame. The assignment: Think of five good things your father gave you throughout your childhood. I insisted to her that my father did not and could not give me anything during my childhood because he was in and out of jail most of my life. She reminded me that Daddy was not locked up for the long bid until I was 16, so I had to think past the incarceration trauma and search for good things my father gave me. If I didn't find those good things, my children and I were destined to carry on this dysfunctional parental relationship. I would be destined to have disappointment and failure in my relationships with men…Whatever!!??

"Money, he gave me lots of money!" I declared.  The therapist looks at me with a disdainful glance and turns her head towards the window. Staring at the skyline she asks, "Anything else?"

"Nope", I snapped.

"OK! " She asserted and closed her journal "Let's pick back up after you have time to give it a deep dive."

"A deep dive? I questioned.

"Yes, the type of healing we are seeking is not on the surface LJ. You have to actually clear the lens in which you view your father so you can see other aspects of his contributions to your life that had a positive impact, but right now all you can see is shade. I'll see you back when you have your list together so we can chat about it." That conversation was eight months ago. Maybe another visit to the prison might help, the last 7 visits didn't.

The drive up to see Daddy is familiar. The thoroughfare is beautiful but sometimes dangerous.  I'm riding with Zion and Zen, my twin cousins. We are two and a half hours drive northwest of Philadelphia where Daddy lives. His rap sheet is almost as long as toilet paper roll. Most of the Garfield brothers have served hard time at some point. Six of seven boys incarcerated for long bids had to be disappointing for a mother. I wonder how Grandmother Mamie did it. Sometimes we joke about my dad and the uncles   competing to see who can get arrested the most times, but it is never really funny, it's just how we discussed it without being overly emotional about it.

The drive today may take us four hours because there is construction, plus there are always falling rocks. Yes, falling rocks! The warning signs are posted at different intervals along the route. State Correctional Institution Uncle Tom is nestled in the Appalachian Mountains. Philly is too, but the further north you travel, the steeper the mountains are in the good 'ol keystone state. Gravity weighs the stones of the mountains down just like it does us, tugging and pulling until we droop and eventually fall off like the rocks.

We left the house; made it to City Line Avenue which turns into 76 West. This part of the drive is still city like- congestion, professional buildings and residential areas. After thirty minutes or so we exit on 476 North. This is a two-lane toll road known as the Pennsylvania Turnpike or PATP. It takes us into the deeper parts of the mountains with no road lights and limited rest stops. The GPS says we are about 100 miles to the exit. I get my ticket from the automatic dispenser and speed off. The girls giggle about the acceleration jerking them back into the plush leather seats of the A8. We don't really talk on these types of drives. We load a fire ass play list and zone out. *Long distance driving is threptic for me,* especially if there is good scenery. I do visualization meditations while I drive. I have to be careful because I've gotten speeding tickets in the past. Zion usually shops for work outfits and accessories. Zen studies for her MCAT. She actually may become a doctor if she stops smoking weed. She pulls out a VooPoo and shares with Zen. Her lil uppity vape is oute with Sarvarski crystals flanking the edges. They puff, puff pass and seventy-five minutes later we are deep in the mountains headed towards US22, which will lead us to Daddy and Uncle Timmy, the twins' father.

The steep winding roads in this area were paved through the rugged terrain leaving jagged edges that climb the mountain elevations but smooth out some in the valleys. Gravity continues tugs at the elevated perimeter causing rocks to fall on the roads below obliterating anything in its way... cars, buildings, people, animals. When it happens, the townsfolk are always talking about it. You hear gossip in the gas stations, grocery stores, restaurants- everywhere. It's interesting to me that the townspeople seem more surprised when falling rock events happen than remorseful for their neighbors hit by the rocks. We have to *plan strategically* when embarking on these journeys to visit the male patriarchs of the family, so as not to become the talk of the town because we were hit by boulders.

This is especially true when we visit in the summer, heat causes the rock to expand allowing it to crumble and collapse onto the roads. In the winter, heaviness caused by the winter cold, snow and ice triggers mini avalanches of snow and boulders. Most of the snow and rocks fall into the river below but it covers the roads in its path.  It is also particularly hazardous when the roads and bridges freeze over. Uphill driving is an obstacle course requiring *advanced maneuvering driving* around stalled vehicles in the roadway and the Department of Transportation trucks clearing ice, snow, rocks and salting the roads. Downhill driving is a slip and slide with many travelers colliding into the guardrail or worse. Some poor losers slide off the cliffs into the snow-covered brushwood at the river's bank. Luckily today is a beautiful autumn day with none of those types of hazards, just construction.. Autumn definitely is the best time of year to go see our family; no snow, no ice, less hazards but same delays.

We chose to go on a weekday because the weekend visitation lines are insane, and we can hardly get a full day's visit in. Today is a sunny day in late September. As I drive, the sunroof is open allowing the natural aroma of high-altitude air to tantalize and sting our nostrils simultaneously.  The climate is breezy and mild...maybe 67 degrees. It reminds me of my Father's homeland, *Jamaica. I have only visited there twice*, but the splashes of color on the shrubbery and trees are similar this time of year. The leaves seem to be dancing in the gentle wind and are a stunning pumpkin color with hints of buttercup, straw, and marigold.

They sway gracefully causing me to stare, but not too long. The thickets along the sides of the road adjacent to the mountain divert my attention. The hues vary from apple green to evergreen to jade. They look lush and healthy, divinely manicured. The snaking road runs parallel to the winding Schuylkill River, or, as parallel as it can be. It's like the river and the roads are racing and the river is in the lead. I can hear the water gushing below. It ripples, splashes, swishes and splatters on the rocks. A light mist sprinkles my face as I accelerate, determined not to let the waterway win today. The girls giggle some more about the mist peppering their bodies and leaving small beads of vapor on our faces. The *sound of the water and the moisture soothe us* and we can't help but be happy…until the red light interrupts our vibe. Shuffle mode changes the song on the playlist as if on que and Benny Goodman's Sing Sing Sing is playing *jazz in the background and it helps maintain my pleasant mood.* I turn it up. Zen gives a sigh of disapproval. She hates jazz, but me and Zion love the drum line and the horns. Zen pops in her ear buds.

I thumb my fingers on the steering wheel and bob my head in sheer enjoyment of the energetic music. Zion shimmies while she shops. Daddy and Uncle both love Benny. We grew up listening to him, Monk, Basie and Coltrane; one of the advantages of growing up with grandparents in the home. The jazz musicians are on the playlist to accompany us on this long ride every time we come. The temperature on the car thermometer reads 65 degrees, I was close. 9:43am. We've been on the road since eight, we're making good time. The music is drowning out the sounds of the river but not the smell of the air. *I love that fresh air smell, that feeling in my nose.* I take another deep breath, and another. Zion syncs her breath with me. Zen somehow does too. We just breathe and enjoy the vibe together but in our own complimentary space. If some of the other cousins were here, they would want to talk and lament over having to drive up here in the first place. We *accept this is a part of our life and we make* it work as best we can while striving to do better.

This ride used to depress me when I first started visiting Daddy. Now *I enjoy the scenery, the air, the river mist, the time alone to think and reflect, being away from work, kids, stress.* The drive is definitely therapeutic. I got to be alone during the drive once a week and I *enjoyed the "me time"* or in this case "cousin time".  The ride was my Thursday ritual for sixteen years, and it grew to be one of my favorite times of the week back then. I had Daddy all to myself and he had me. Today, I share this ritual with my cousins so we can see my uncle too.  Just at that moment a single golden leaf drifts into my sunroof.  Zion shoos the leaf like it is a fly or something then it lands on my lap. I admire it while waiting at the traffic light.  The texture is smooth and cool against my fingers.  Damp… Beep! Beep! Hoooonk! The truck behind us interrupted my thoughts, rushing me to go through the intersection. The light is green. I pause before I accelerate checking the rear view and letting all the windows down in my sedan. My cousins get ready. The wind is blowing strong now as if reinforcing the drama that may unfold. It is tossing my locs like I'm in a drop top convertible. Zion puts a ball cap on while Zen eyeballs the driver in the truck speeding up to go around us. The Red Ram truck plows past us, honking, and the driver gives us the finger. I smile at him, and we all return the gesture. I honk the horn to some tune of Art Blakely I don't know the name of. The next red light forces us to meet again. We all scowl at the Bubba looking dude in overalls and a cowboy hat. He returns the glare and displays his rifle like a crossbody bag. We *present our arms* in return, Zion cocks her pistol and points it at him, ninety degrees. Side grip baby! Surprised, Bubba races off before the light turns green and makes a hard left on Bunker Hill drive. The odds weren't in his favor, nor ours, but especially not his, it could have been bad. Zen made note of his license plate as we continued our journey satisfied with our baby girl gangster moves. No one giggled at nor talked about the encounter. We are our fathers' kids for sure, we r*espect the weapons and trained to defend ourselves*. I love my cousins and we all knew displaying your weapon is a threat. We were silent the rest of the ride.

We make a right on Orerro Lane. The street is steep. We are almost there so I look in the mirror of the visor; my face is still damp from the river mist.  I allow the moisture to seep into my skin as I apply a fresh coat of lip gloss. I put the leaf in the visor for good luck, head still bobbing with the drums.  Clarinet therapy is levitating my mood higher than the jagged edges of the mountain side. The sun is beaming through the roof; breeze allowing the leaves to dance and the wind flowing through my hair. I breathe it all in. This would be a perfect day if we weren't going to jail.

I pulled into a spot several rows back from the entrance and asked the girls to sign us in while I made a phone call and put our stuff in the trunk. I need to check in with my TA to make sure there are no issues with the classes and lock up our purses. We can only enter the visiting room with keys and money. They walk off telling me to hurry up. I finish the call and lock the car and walk in with a small backpack and a jacket. The visitation room is cold year-round. I walk immediately to the storage area. I put the backpack in the locker but not the jacket. Observing the waiting room I see Zen is chatting with other families visiting and Zion is watching me. I stick my tongue out at her and roll my eyes. She shakes her head and flags me to come to her. I insert the coins, turn and release the locker key. I sashay over to Zion and plop down next to her and sit with my cousins and the other family members who volunteered to go to jail to see their loved ones.

The attempts for candid conversation with my father did not go so well. He kept hugging me and hanging on me. He did not want to discuss his incarceration or the effects it has on me, his grandchildren and the rest of the family. He refused to acknowledge that when the father is caged the entire family is held in captivity. He just wanted to enjoy our "family" day and adhere to his vision for the visit. I reluctantly agreed because who wants to drive four hours to argue? We *played spades,* dominoes, and ate vending machine food and pretended this was a normal family bonding. We even took some pictures before the visitation hours ended. Daddy gave me a long, big hug and told me he loved me then mugged the back of my head. It was like he attached himself to me through our embrace. I giggled at his playfulness. We finished our goodbyes and I asked Zen to drive back to Philly. She agreed. We made our way through the sector doors, then the detention doors back to the visitor's waiting room. We all made a bathroom stop before we hit the road. We exited the building walking towards the car, hopped in and Zen started the engine. I sat in the back observing the visitors departing. There was a long line of cars waiting to leave the parking lot moving slower than usual. We waited a few minutes to decide when to pull off, but we saw other cars taking another exit we were not familiar with. Zion qued the music, I checked Waze and found another route with less traffic saving 30 minutes on the ride home, Zen cuts in the traffic line triggering a symphony of horns and swares. We all laughed understanding the irritation of being cut off but… it was necessary! I like that we *work together as a team*, a unit, a posse.

It was still nice outside as we took the back roads to the turnpike. About thirty minutes into our drive I rolled down my window to *enjoy the scenery of nature* as the sun began to set. *I love the crisp mountain air.* The leaf I saved earlier slipped from the visor and gently flew into my face. The wind gently pressed it into my skin, catching my eyelashes. I took it between my fingers and looked at it wondering why Daddy could not talk to me. Feeling a wave of emotion I looked up to see Zen smiling at me through the driver visor mirror. She winked at me and closed the mirror as if saying "it's going to be OK cousin." Geez I hope so, I thought! I guess I wanted My father to tell me what he thought he taught me, to give me an explanation, an apology, after the hugs and kisses, reassurance that he loved me or something. I felt like I needed his perspective and Daddy was avoiding the topic because he know what I knew…that he didn't teach me ish!

Hot, angry and sad tears began to stream down my face making me feel nauseous. I felt like I was going to vomit. I sat in the back seat crying silently feeling the heaviness of resenting my father. The lump in my throat made it hard for me to breathe. My nose began to run and I just let the purge begin without holding it in. I folded my body over placing my head between my legs, trying to breathe but all I could do was moan in pain and disappointment trying not to throw up. I couldn't stop crying. The moaning turned into a low pitched wailing. I tried to regain my composure but my eyes were tightening and the lump seemed to be getting bigger. I began to hyperventilate. It felt like the presence of an absent father was clenching my throat and gripping my soul right out of my body! WTF is happening to me?!

Zen quickly pulled over at a scenic rest stop then hopped out of the car. She came around and opened my door and helped me as I fell out of the car. The prison food exploded from my mouth like something you see in B rated horror movies. It was gross. I felt like everything I ate for the last three weeks was just ejected from my mouth. I was glad Zion was asleep or she would tease me about this emotional episode as I am the oldest cousin. I slumped against the car and sat on the ground. I could feel the coolness of *the earth begin to immediately ground me* through my jeans. I let out a huge sigh and laid in the grass away from the vomit. I began to mumble the serenity prayer while tears continued to trail my face. Zen was confused, just looking at me with a glare-stare. She didn't know what to do so she just sat beside me on mute and began to roll a joint.

"Lord grant me the serenity to accept the things I can not change (my father). The courage to change the things I can (myself), and the wisdom to know the difference (acceptance)". I did not know the rest of the prayer but I really was trying to live one day at a time; enjoying one moment at a time; while taking this world as it is and not as I would have it but I was struggling. I still was trusting that God would make all things right and I believed if I surrendered to the Creator's will I may be reasonably happy in this life and supremely happy with God and the ancestors forever in the next. But, this emotional episode was the reality of the gap in my ability and my faith. I kept praying and Zen kept puffing. It was like a puff, puff, pray because I don't smoke. I rolled over to lay on my cousin's lap. My heavy head rested on her legs. Still sobbing. She remained quiet, but she put her arm around me and we watched the sunset as it disappeared behind the mountain bluff.

I woke up to Zion shaking me and telling me to get up and get out of the car. A little disoriented I looked around. We were at my mom's house. How did I get back in the car? What time is it? Who cares? I took a deep breath as I shifted my weight to ready myself to exit the car. I don't know if Zen slept through my curbside meltdown or if Zion told her to shut up about it, but either way I was grateful she wasn't talking trash about my sensitivity to me and daddy's situation. I gave them both a hug and walked slowly towards the house. As Zen pulls off, I hear Zion say "Moving to Houston has made your ass soft cousin." I turn to see Zen playfully hit her. I didn't have my usually snappy comeback, so I disappeared into the dark sanctuary of mommy's driveway feeling like Zion was right. Tears began to stream again.

I don't know how long I was sitting in the dark before my grandmother wandered into the kitchen and turned on the light. I must have startled her because she screamed and swatted at me. I blocked her and dryly said "Granny, it's me!" She glared at me, shaking her fist at me, then smiled and sat down beside me. She was clasping her hands like prayer time and began slowly rocking back and forth studying me.

"What's the matter sweetie? Why are you so sad?"

"I'm ok Granny."

"You don't look ok lil girl and God told me to come down here and get you together."

"Oh yeah?, I replied sarcastically. "I am OK Granny, this too shall pass."

"Do you think sitting in the dark will make it pass faster?"

"Nope!" I laughed.

"Well, I am here. Why don't you give it to me sweetie."

My grandmother had always been a good listener, so I reluctantly began to share with her how I was trying to think of five good things my father gave me throughout my childhood but I couldn't think of any. The dumb therapist was making me do this dumb assignment. I went to see him in prison today as I had on a regular basis for almost half my life and he would not even discuss it with me; he just wanted us to visit in peace but I wasn't at peace. I told her about how I lost out on jobs because I could not get security clearance because of HIS record.

"Is there anything else", she asked?

YES!  He knows how relationships with men have been a struggle for me my whole life and he doesn't help me navigate. How I have three children by three different fathers who all loved me deeply but could not survive my unhealed trauma in our relationship. Trauma caused by him. How I have trust issues, abandonment issues, self esteem issues.

"Is there anything else", she asked again?

"Yes!" I went on and on and on complaining about every egregious action and non action I could think of. I don't know how long I lamented but Granny was attentive, nodding, looking into my eyes, wiping my tears and holding my hand. She had a tender look on her face of understanding and compassion. I was beginning to feel better. She gave me a big hug and rocked me for a few moments. Much better.

I got up and began to make some tea for us as I continued to have diarrhea of the mouth about daddy's oblivion to my pain, disappointment and resentment. Then at some point I was done. I just stopped talking. Granny was silent with a gentle twinkling grin.

We remained quiet for several moments. My gaze drifted to the sky outside Mommy's bay windows. The pinks and plums and baby blues stirred gratitude in my spirit. The sun was rising and so was I. My head returned to behold my grandmother! Oh! She was glorious! Granny looked at me and she smiled at me and she said to me "Did you enjoy the ride?"

"What", I replied feeling a bit confused, sipping my cold tea. "Did I enjoy the ride?"

"Did you enjoy the ride?" Feeling annoyance creeping back in, I said "yes".

"Well good Keeta Bug. Why don't you just start there?"

It was that tender moment with my grandmother that helped shift the lens in which I viewed my father Granny's simplistic wisdom then, is profound to me now. Daddy has taught me so many things that I did not recognize for decades. Some of which I have italicized in this story, others I will save for another story. So, needless to say I was finally able to complete the task my therapist gave me even though it took me almost two years to do it. During the process I also learned some things about myself.

A wise person told me that feelings buried alive never die, they haunt you. I had to ponder that for some time. I now understand how my buried feelings about my father have haunted me in all of my romantic relationships so the relationships died. The resentment I had for my father created a huge grudge towards him that transferred to the men I was dating and I wasn't even aware of it. I had no clue. That Daddy grudge was part of the reason I had so much difficulty doing the assignment the therapist gave me.

I learned from that assignment the therapist gave me that holding a grudge against your parents is a curse. Not a curse in the sense of some supernatural power that inflicts harm or punishment upon the intended but more like an affliction of the spirit. An afflicted spirit holds a very specific perspective that causes them harm and oftentimes causes their loved ones harm too.

The begrudged parent curse has been in my family for at least five generations. I am the third generation. I have passed it to my eldest son who has passed it to his only daughter. As my father's only child, my assignment is to reverse the curse~ which is to remove my affliction~ remove my dysfunctional perspective causing me harm…causing my family harm. So… this divine assignment was to fully forgive my father and to help my son forgive me, so my granddaughter can forgive him. I had to learn Daddy's life journey was not mine to forgive. It was a sacred agreement between him and God. Who am I to judge?? Daddy had a right to live his life however he chose based on the lessons he had to learn, not based on how I felt about it. My son has to learn that my life's journey is not his to forgive. I have the right to live my life however I choose based on the lessons I have to learn, not based on how he feels about it. It's a huge pill of a lesson, I know. It literally took me decades to find the good in Daddy. Because I held that grudge for most of my life it became a part of my identity and it was hard for me to let that go. But, I did and we must if we are to heal.

Sometimes I reread the completed assignment the therapist had me do to keep my forgiveness fresh. My love for long distance driving is a direct result of driving to see Daddy over the years. My defensive driving ability is too, because I had to learn to maneuver the roads in the icy, snowy mountains. The feel and smell of cold, fresh air in my nose is a sensation I love because of my visiting my father in the mountains! Daddy loved jazz and he shared his love for that music with me. I play all sorts of cognitive games thatI learned during my visits with my father: spades, pinochle, pokeno, dominos, chess, checkers, solitaire. That's five right there! Using nature to ground me, learning targeted prayers, and enjoying time to myself are all skills Daddy taught me to keep me emotionally balanced. Daddy made sure I was a good markswoman. He supported my mother's decisions on how to raise me and made sure we were properly funded even when he was in jail. The list of good things Daddy gave me goes on; and to think for the longest I just saw him as a common criminal, a thug~ not a highly influential Black activist that the government needed to neutralize. My father introduced me to Black nationalism and I never acknowledged him or thanked him for that philosophy.

My father believed that he had to do his part to liberate Black people from the insanity of racism in this country. He really believed it was a part of his personal mission to be the thorn in the system's side, all six foot eight of him. He enjoyed the fear he evoked in white people, but he did not enjoy it as much when he scared Black people or the people he was trying to help but he understood it came with the territory. He was a generous and loving man especially to his family. He was passionate and strategic, visionary and coordinating with his activist peers. Daddy was intelligent with a good sense of humor. He was a cooperative leader who developed other leaders. His projects funded many of the RBG, Black art, Muslim, Isrealites, and other Black empowerment movements in Philly in the '70's, 80's and early 90's. Institutions that still stand today because of his input and sacrifice. Daddy was a viable threat and a formidable adversary to anyone who stood in the way of his mission, free man or imprisoned, as his reach was long and wide. He instilled many of those traits into me as his relationship with me was one of the greatest sacrifices he made for a cause he believed in. In his quest to help undo the curse of racism in our national family he unwittingly carried on a curse in his biological family.

I am his only known legacy as he has been a ghostwriter in so many pages of Philadelphian urban history so, now it is my assignment to reverse the curse. Let us begin!

### My Role Model, My Sister's Love~ Tonnia Cotton

It's nothing like having a sister that truly loves you. Relationships like that give you someone that really loves you and you can love them back. My sister has always been one that I looked up to and respected, I always knew she had my back. The day she called and told me that she was in the hospital, I dropped what I was doing at work and made it to the hospital. The last thing I thought was she was really sick, let alone dying. Our bond changed forever after that phone call.

When I arrived at the hospital I was so nervous walking towards her room. I remember that hospital smell. You know the one, some call it a sterile smell or an antiseptic smell. I was not concerned at first, but as I got closer to her room I noticed what machines she was on, that smell of fear came upon me. Then I saw all the sad faces, maybe the smell was sadness or grief. I continued to her room, number 227. When I found it, I stopped, took a deep breath, said a quick prayer and opened the door with the best cheerful smile I could muster.

As I walked into the room I was immediately stopped by a nurse. She informed me that I needed to wait a few moments before she was ready for family. Thank God! I will take a beat to get myself together. My brother-in-law came out to check on me but wouldn't give me all the details, so I knew it was bad. I told myself I am good, my sister is good, we will be good.

A short while later I was allowed in the room to visit my sister. When we walked in I saw a look in her eyes that made me understand the seriousness of her hospitalization and tears welled up in my eyes before she could tell me what's wrong. I immediately hugged her and held her tight in my arms. I rocked her back and forth for several moments before she began to speak.

She shared with me that she had terminal liver disease, that she needed a liver transplant, that she had 60 to 90 days to live if she did not get that liver transplant. She believed that she was about to die. I believed that God would find a way to help my sister live.

Have you ever heard a message that impacted you so much that you felt like you were dreaming? This news was more like a nightmare. After she shared her diagnosis with me all I could do was look out the window of the hospital room. A life flight helicopter was landing, bringing another poor soul with a terminal medical condition to this place. I swallowed hard trying to hold back my tears. She's not even 60 yet! How can this be happening?

I immediately started asking questions, probing questions that made the medical staff explain our situation again and again. I noticed concern in my sister's face and I relented. I looked at my brother-in-law and I made a decision that it was time to shift from the pity party into action. All my life my sister was assigned duties. She helped raise me, but now I had this assignment. I remember telling my sister we were going to run this race against the clock together.

Truthfully it was one of the scariest things I ever experienced. Thank God my husband accepted his assignment and he took care of me so I could take care of my sister. Every day for 60-plus days my hubby drove me to the hospital. I had to walk into that hospital room with a smile on my face as I watch my sister get weaker and weaker. I prayed and cried out to God, I screamed many nights in the car on the way home. I sang Tasha Cobb's song, "He knows my name"... every day and cried out to God. Imagine watching your sister's strength become so weak she could not hold a mobile phone in her hand. I am not a nurse but my assignment was to help my brother-in-law be a caretaker. My assignment was to make sure my niece was a part of every decision and pray for her daily. My sister has one gorgeous daughter, and they are best friends. I was scared because I know they talk every day. I remember asking questions to the doctors and nurses. I remember asking one doctor to step out of my sister's room in the hall. I told her that it made no sense that she walked into the room. telling my sister she was sick. I was like she knows she is sick but why are you speaking such negative words? I shared with the doctor the God I serve can do anything he wants. My assignment was to protect my sister the same way she protected me. I took this assignment seriously.

I remember calling the chef that did my meal prep and asking if he could help. I wanted to do anything I could to help my brother-in-law as we waited for a liver. My sister was released to go home but I kept praying. I was worried about my niece and mom. My god sister taking care of Mom. My assignment was to become strong, but I needed help, God sent it. When my  firstborn son began asking questions about how to get her the help she needed, what we needed to do, how much was it going to cost; that pushed me into problem solving mode. When I had conversations with my baby girl, who was living in Nebraska at the time, and came home to support me allowed me to become the pillar for the family. One Sunday when my spirits were low I lost it at church. I ran to the altar and cried my soul out. Our first lady met me at the altar and whispered "Tonnia, God got you, He is going to work a miracle. He is using this time to strengthen you!" She was assigned to me that day. When I reflected back I realized so many people stepped into their assignments to support me, to support my sister.

I knew I could not replace my sister's contribution to our family but I surely was not going to be weak. I remember one day she told me she wanted to go home when she was in the hospital. I thought she meant the house, but she meant heaven. I looked at her in the face and said, "You remember running track? We are going to run this race together. We are about to run the 4x4, are you ready?"

God knows I was scared, but I knew God was going to protect and guide me. I had to be strong, meanwhile watching my sister suffer. One night I had to try and warm her up while she just shook. I hurt to see her hurt but it was my assignment to be with her. Then, the day I walked into the hospital room and I could smell death ever so clearly. It wasn't like the first day I walked into her hospital room. I was not giving up. She watched me to see how I was going to react. I watched my niece drive back and forth to Dallas. I watched my niece pass out after driving from Dallas to Houston. My heart was so heavy; I would call her on the phone and hear the heart. I would try and keep a happy force while on the phone. Then crying after being on the phone.

Then, that day, in October! The call came informing us that a liver match for my sister was identified. We had to prepare for emergency surgery. It was a long surgery. We sat in that waiting room, praying, crying, and listening to Tasha Cobbs songs on repeat. We continued to get updates from the surgical team. When she is out of surgery; I just praised God. We walked into the room and I knew we had a long way to go. I immediately whispered to her, "Hey you ready to run this race?" My brother-in-law, niece, nephew, children, husband, god sister, aunt, and I all had assignments to help my sister be alive.

My sister is a fighter but when she came out of surgery, I did not recognize her! She was so swollen when they wheeled her out. Thank God, I did not show my fear. I am a believer, she is a believer and the village that surrounded her was beyond believing and praying. We had faith and we realized that our assignments had changed throughout these 90 days so we could receive a miracle. In those days after the surgery, I sang to her during her recovery. I played her favorite songs. I did what was needed for her to feel loved and supported. I "showed up".

Years later and my sister continues to live and progress. Just know God knows your name. He has assignments for you no matter how the situation looks. God has plans to prosper us Jeremiah 29:11. We must be still to understand the assignment. We must be aligned with reading our word, praying, and surrounding ourselves with people that are not your little god but people that have the same beliefs. An assignment from God may come with joy and struggles. But you must believe that no weapons form against you shall prosper. Pray about your assignment. The reward will come with a peace of knowing he never left you through the assignment. Satan tries to fool us. He gives assignments that make you feel like you got what you wanted. But, you did it; not God; but you did it! He gives you that feel good assignment. His assignment where you may be used to destroy someone else with your words or your actions. His assignment comes with selfish motives. Be careful. Pray and be wise. Genesis 50:20.

**The Forgiveness Letter**

**Ephesians 4:20**

**~Mrs. Germain Jackson Eddie**

**"Be kind and compassionate to one another,**

**forgiving each other, just as in Christ God has forgiven you!"**

My assignment in this part of my life is to learn how to activate forgiveness for the most heinous cat another can commit. It has taken me a long time to get to this point but it started with me writing a forgiveness letter to the person who murdered my only child Melvin Joseph Maxwell, Jr.

August 17, 1983, Hurricane Alicia made landfall and changed the course of my life forever. Alicia did not devastate my family directly at the time but she set in motion a chain of events that has caused me overwhelming pain. She also took the lives of 21 others, injured 7,500 Houstonians and caused over $3 billion dollars in damage in her path.

I remember the day Alicia hit, she was more wind than she was water. At the time I was a young newlywed almost three years into marriage and seven months pregnant. We lived in Humble, so our area was not directly impacted by the storm, but the city and surrounding areas were shut down for a few days. It took years for the city to fully recover and the beach erosion from the storm still impacts Galveston vegetation to this day.

When the city reopened, I caught the Park and Ride bus to work. I loved my job at the Commercial Bank downtown. I was one of the few black people that worked there. When I got off the bus, I was shocked that a lot of downtown buildings were destroyed. I could see glass was still falling from the high- rise buildings on our commute in. There was so much debris in the streets that it was deemed unsafe to walk above ground. The bus driver dropped us off at an underground tunnel entrance to walk to our respective buildings. Before I descended into the tunnels I paused to look around. I felt like I was witnessing the ends of the earth. Chunks of the buildings and glass were strewn as far as I could see, cars overturned, trees snapped in two, total destruction was all around us and the bank was back to business as usual. My belly tightened as I fought back my emotions. Cleaning crews had not made it to McKinney Street, so I slowly walked down the stairs to the underground passageway to the bank. I did not realize the stress and strain of seeing that type of devastation going to work had on me until I went into labor four days later.

I was so stressed out managing our home, distressed family members and neighbors, backed up claims and payroll at work and that I gave birth to my son five weeks early. Melvin Joseph Maxwell, Jr., was born on August 21, 1983 at the hospital downtown close to my job. He was three pounds and three ounces born at 3:33AM. My heart was filled with joy. It was love at first sight; he was so tiny but he was a fighter. Melvin was on a ventilator for several weeks and lived in an incubator the first three months of his life. I could not take him home right away because his lungs were not fully developed and he needed to gain some weight. We visited him everyday. By Thanksgiving he was stronger and by Christmas he came home. The love and attention from the family helped Melvin grow even stronger. By the spring we had a baby shower to celebrate his progress. I remember he slept through the entire gathering as he was passed from one loving family member to the next. We were celebrating his life.

Melvin had a typical southern childhood filled with ice cream and hot summers. He didn't look like a preemie any more. He was big, strong and handsome like his father. In 1988 we had him baptized at a Baptist Church in Houston. He served as a boy scout and junior usher. Then, he became a member of a Baptist Church in Beaumont, Texas in 1995. Most recently, he was a member of World Mission Society Church of God in Beaumont, where he remained a member Texas until his death.

Melvin graduated from High School in 2001 in Beaumont, Texas. Later, he graduated from an Institute of Technology in 2005 in Beaumont, Texas with an Associate Degree in Welding. Melvin worked as a worker in various refineries in Beaumont and Port Arthur, Texas. Melvin married both of his high school sweethearts, at different times of course, but who does that? He did!

Each marriage produced four children. He fathered three more children outside of his marriage by other women, so I have seven beautiful grandchildren. As you can see, his relationship with women was… complicated at best and I won't pretend to have all the details, but what I do know is he did not deserve to die alone, abandoned in a cheap motel room, regardless of how complicated it was. Now that you have some background, let's get back to my forgiveness story.

On August 17, 2017, Hurricane Harvey made landfall, devastating Port Arthur, Texas and other areas. The storm waters flooded all over Port Arthur and neighboring communities. We were evacuated from our homes by helicopters to neighboring cities and states. My husband, eldest granddaughter and I were evacuated to Lake Charles, Louisiana and stayed there for a week. During that time, Melvin stayed in Dallas, Texas for two weeks. One of my friends who was staying with family in Lake Charles drove us back to Port Arthur, Texas to assess the damage after the waters subsided. When we arrived, our home was flooded out and deemed unlivable. We lost everything. Melvin's trailer home was flooded too. We did not qualify to stay in a hotel using a FEMA voucher because we exceeded the income requirements. We needed to figure something out and figure it out quickly! Thank God a friend helped us out and ame to the rescue. We stayed with my former supervisor in Beaumont, Texas for nine months. Melvin was blessed and was granted a FEMA voucher to stay in a hotel while the insurance claim was processed. At first Melvin getting FEMA gave me peace of mind but he lacked stability in an already tumultuous situation.

Melvin stayed in hotels in Orange, Port Arthur and Houston, Texas, bouncing wherever FEMA would pay for. But, we had our own challenges. Our insurance did not cover damages to our home because we did not have flood insurance. We did not know food insurance was a whole different insurance policy. However, Melvin had flood insurance on his trailer home. I filed an insurance claim on the trailer and received a check in the mail for $10,000.00. Things seemed like they were turning around. I planned to use the money to purchase Melvin another trailer and reimburse my friend for living expenses during our stay in Beaumont.  I searched the internet for another trailer home to purchase for Melvin. I found a great trailer deal on eBay. I emailed the seller's my interest in purchasing the trailer. We settled on a price of $6, 500.00 dollars. I was so excited that we were getting back on track after this trauma.

The seller informed me that before he would ship the trailer to Melvin's trailer park, I had to pay for the trailer. I arranged for full payment using eBay debit cards.  I paid $6,500 to the sellers for the trailer and received the shipping information via email that the trailer was scheduled to arrive in one week from the payment. We began purchasing items for Melvin's home feeling blessed.

One week had elapsed and the trailer had not arrived yet. At first, I was not worried because we had survived a major catastrophe so we expected delays. I began to call the seller but he did not respond. I emailed the seller, still no response. After three weeks of the seller not returning my emails or calls I began to worry. I kept calling and emailing not wanting to give up hope. Then it happened. The phone number I was calling was disconnected. I called eBay to report the fraudulent purchase.  EBay did not have a record of me purchasing a trailer.  Turns out I was dealing with a fake eBay website.  I lost $6,500.00 to a scam.

I thought the situation could not get any worse but it did.  Melvin broke up with his girlfriend who was pregnant with who is now his youngest son. His ex-girlfriend evacuated with her family to Galveston, Texas.  While she was staying there, she gave birth to a baby boy on November 6, 2017. Because they were broken up, her parents would not allow Melvin to visit his ex or their baby boy in the hospital in Galveston. When she and the baby were released from the hospital they moved to Vidor, Texas. Her family still would not allow Melvin to visit his newborn son and I never really understood why. He only had pictures of his son on his cell phone that were texted to him by his son's mother.  Needless to say, Melvin never got a chance to visit or hold his son. I found out later that the woman claimed Melvin was aggressive towards her so she was fearful of what he may say or do. I have never known Melvin to be aggressive to me or any women for that matter.

On November 22, 2017, Melvin moved to Houston, Texas to stay with his aunt.  He continued processing his FEMA claim for a permanent place to stay.  He celebrated Thanksgiving, Christmas and New Year's with his aunt and his father's side of the family. As he interacted with the family at gatherings, Melvin met another woman.  This woman also had seven children.  They started dating each other. On January 4, 2018, Melvin  called me to tell me he was traveling to Nederland, Texas with his new girlfriend for a doctor's visit to refill his pills prescription.  Melvin was dealing with some mental health issues as a result of the trauma in the storm and needed his anxiety medication.When Melvin does not have his medication he can have episodes of depression and isolation.His new girlfriend seems to help him with the episodes and I was glad she was going with him to the doctor's appointment. That was the last day I spoke to my son.

I understood that sometimes Melvin would disappear for days or weeks if he is having an episode because he does not want to be bothered. So when I did not hear from him for a couple weeks I was not overly concerned. I called him and left a few voicemails but he did not return my call. Soon I began to worry. On January 20, 2018, I was notified by Melvin's father that during Melvin's stay in a Houston hotel, he was murdered by his girlfriend. She stabbed him to death and he was left in the hotel room with a do not disturb sign on the door. He told me that Melvin had been dead for two weeks before they found him because the room was paid in advance by the voucher and it was not being serviced by housekeeping. It wasn't until the month's voucher was due that hotel personnel checked on the room and even then they did not enter the room.

Melvin's childhood friend, with the help of the Houston Police Department, found him dead with a knife broken off in his chest. His body was so severely decomposed, the morgue needed dental records to identify Melvin. This news was so disturbing to me I was in a state of shock. I did not believe it. It was like a crime story reality show. I was so devastated I couldn't even cry, not once, tears would not flow. All I could do is pray to the Lord that He will comfort me and my family during this bereavement period.

At the time of Melvin's death, we were still homeless, staying with my former supervisor. Instead of me going to Houston to identify the body, his father did it. I was so blessed to know one of my best friends from Beaumont whose husband and his family are owners of a funeral home. The staff drove to Houston  to bring Melvin's body to Beaumont where it was cremated. Melvin's father arranged for his brother's limousine service to pick up and drop off five of Melvin's children, my husband, my mother-in-law and I for Melvin's homegoing service. It was held Saturday, January 27, 2018 at a Baptist Church in Houston, Texas.  Melvin's grandfather, Pastor of a Baptist Church in Jasper, Texas officiated and delivered the eulogy. My Pastor, Assistant Pastor and church members from my Baptist Church in Port Arthur  attended the funeral.  My family, friends, classmates, co-workers and boss also attended the funeral service.  My father looked at me and said, "Germain, Melvin was a real grandson!" Then he said to me, "Well Done!" During a solo rendered by my brother who is a Preacher, "Anchor in the Lord".  That's when I suddenly started crying uncontrollably. I fell to the floor and laid out with tears of sadness. My husband helped me get off the floor and I gathered my composure.  I remembered, six of Melvin's children who were attending his homegoing service were watching me.  I have to be strong for my grandchildren. After service, we held a red and black balloon release in front of the church. Melvin's repast was held at a banquet room in Houston by Melvin's father's relatives. Thank God for my biological father, he had an insurance policy on Melvin. The insurance policy covered the funeral service and cremation.  I ordered urns for Melvin's parents, grandparents and urn pennants for his children.

My seven grandchildren~ four boys and three girls' lives were impacted forever. One of my granddaughters, My'reaka, I was raising suffered depression and sadness during her bereavement period. We were still staying with my former supervisor at the time.  She would go into her room closet to cry. I would console her and reassure her that God loves her. God won't put more on us than we can bear.  She attended counseling sessions in Port Neches.  In her church, she attended Sunday school and worship services. She serves on the usher board. Also, she attended a "Position Yourself: The Process for the Progress' ' conference with me which was led by my best friend Tonnia Cotton. I seek to heal for myself and for: My oldest granddaughter, Madalya, My oldest grandson, Montreal, My youngest granddaughter, Mashanna, My youngest grandson, Zy'ion, My next to the oldest grandson, Jasys, My next to the youngest grandson, Chrishaun.

I kept praying and praying and finally, on June 10, 2021 a murder charge was filed in the Harris County Court on Melvin's murderer. Will not say her name but she was arrested and booked in Atlanta, Georgia June 28, 2021. She was returning from being in Jamaica. She was not extradited to Houston, Texas until September 14, 2021.

I attended along with my family, the first court date was on February 17, 2022. Regretfully, nothing was accomplished because the District Attorney requested her recorded confession from when she was booked in Atlanta, Georgia.  I attended the second court date on May 04, 2022. The District Attorney received the recorded confession but the recording was not clear.  They requested a clearer recording of her confession. I attended the third court day on August 3, 2022. During this court hearing, Jane recanted her confession.  She is now saying it was self defense. I attended the fourth court day on November 16, 2022. The District Attorney's office received evidence from cell phone records that contradicts Jane's self defense statement. I attended the fifth Court day on January 31, 2023. Finally the District Attorney and Defense is ready for trial.  The trial date was set for May 12, 2023.

The judicial process is awful and drawn out and I have grown weary of the unfinished trial. My journey of grieving Melvin's death has been very difficult. I experienced bitterness, disparity, depression, emptiness, sadness, hopelessness, hurtfulness, and sorrowfulness.  I was so obsessed with the loss of my son, I was ignoring my husband's call to "get rid of bitterness, rage, and anger, brawling and slander, along with every form of malice." (Ephesians 4:31)  But how? Over time, God revealed three ways to me:

1. Take your Bitterness to Him - Ask Him to banish it.  In reply, I heard God say, "Forgive."  But How?

2. Ask God To Teach You - In fact, forgiveness isn't an act, it's a process. As scholar Lewis Smedes explained, forgiveness doesn't excuse offenders; it means "we are ready to be healed." How?

3. Rely on the Holy Spirit's Great Power - Then His work in us becomes His witness. Indeed, "But you will receive power when the Holy Spirit comes on you; and you will be witnesses to the ends of the earth. (Acts 1:8)

As God does His work for us, a bitter root can bloom in Christ into a beautiful flower.  True, our "soil" will always need weeding. But God's love can turn our bitterness into grace.

Jesus made it clear that forgiveness is powerful.  He said, "If you forgive other people when they sin against you, your heavenly Father will also forgive you."  (Matthew 6:14) Later in answering Peter, Christ told how often we should forgive:  "I tell you, not seven times, but seventy-seven times." (Matthew 18:22) And on the cross, He demonstrated godly forgiveness when He prayed. "Father, forgive them, for they do not know what they are doing." (Luke 23:34)

Forgiveness at its fullest can be realized when both parties move toward healing and reconciliation.  And while it doesn't remove the effects of harm done or the need to be discerning in how to address painful or unhealthy relationships, it can lead to restored one's testifying to God's love and power.  Let's look for ways to "extend forgiveness" for his honor.

In order for me to grow stronger in my spiritual walk, I had to practice the words of the Serenity Prayer: **God grant me the serenity to accept the things I cannot change, courage to change the things I can, and the wisdom to know the difference, living one day at a time; enjoying one moment at a time; taking this world as it is and not as I would have it; trusting that God will make all things right if I surrender to Your will; so that I may be reasonably happy in this life and**

I prayed to God to comfort me and give me peace. I began to study the word of God on forgiveness. I attended my church's worship service on Sundays and mission meetings, prayer meetings and bible studies on Mondays. My Pastor and Assistant Pastor prayed for me and my family. My Pastor anoints my head with oil. (Philippians 4:13) reads, "I can do all things through Christ who strengthens me." God gives me strength to cope with grief and despair. Some of my church members, family, co-workers, classmates and friends shared inspirational and encouraging words with me. I joined a sister support group named "Sisters Supporting Sisters" under the leadership of my best friend, Tonnia Cotton, of Houston, Texas. I started attending her bible studies, workshops and conferences virtually. Now, I was offered an opportunity to join Tonnia and other women to contribute her book titled "Understand Your Assignment." This is the letter I wrote to her.

Dear Jane Doe,

I forgive you for murdering my only son, Melvin Joseph Maxwell, Jr., January 4, 2018 at the Best Western Hotel, in the Galleria, in Houston, Texas. The knife you broke off in his chest after stabbing my son to death not only took his life but left a gaping hole in the lives of his family members. I do not understand why you left him and placed a do not disturb sign on his hotel room door, but I pray for your soul. Tragically, he was not found until January 20, 2018, two weeks after his death. This news was so devastating to me. It's been over five years since we lost our son Melvin. We were not ready for Melvin to leave this earth. But, we know Melvin is in a better place with our Father in Heaven. We and the family miss Melvin so much! We wanted to keep Melvin, but God willed it not to be. Now Melvin is in God's keeping! So dear God, take care of Melvin, until we meet again! We will always love you, Melvin! May Melvin rest in peace in Heaven. May our family continue to heal from this trauma and also find peace.

I have been holding feelings of bitterness, sadness, anger and depression since I lost my son.  Holding on to these feelings have affected me physically and emotionally. The possible difference it could make in my life if I could let these feelings go is I will be able to live stress free.  The fears I have for letting go of these feelings, I will forget my son. You have impacted my entire family.  My son left behind seven children whose names are Madalya, My'reaka, Montreal, Jasys, Mashanna, Chrishaun and Zy'ion. We are hopeful and prayerful that justice will be served. In the bible there is a scripture about forgiving one another.  In Ephesians 4:31-32 it reads King James Version [31] Let all bitterness, and wrath, and anger, and clamor, and evil speaking, be put away from you, with all malice: [32] And be ye kind one to another, tenderhearted, forgiving one another, even as God for Christ's sake hath forgiven you.  With that said, I forgive you for what you have done.  Just as God forgave us.

## Bringing Closure

The stories shared in the booklet are directly experienced from the lives of the co-authors. Some names and places have been changed to protect the privacy of others. We have shared our individual and collective assignments with you for three main reasons:

1. **To remind you that God works** mysteriously and plainly. Understanding your assignments at different times in your life keeps you connected to God and has a huge impact on your family and your community.
2. **To encourage dialogue** about sensitive topics. Start with your close circle of family and friends. The healing may not occur all at once but start the process and keep unpacking the emotional baggage and the load will become lighter.
3. **To inspire healing** the trauma we have experienced in our lives. We all have emotional residue from some distressing events in the past but if we never revisit it to address it from a different perspective it continues to have negative influences over our choices in the present to  give undesirable results in our futures.

These beautiful women all have something in common. They had an assignment that was fulfilled or continues to be fulfilled for God. You too have an assignment to be fulfilled for God. When God gives us assignments it may not be easy. Our Father will be with you through the ups and downs, the trials and tribulations, the fantastic and the devastating. He will never leave you. It's important to remember the Lord is our shepherd, we shall not want. Psalm 121:1. It's  important to remember you must lean not on your understanding but on God's.

Throughout life, it's important that each of us stop and look at life experiences as assignments. We all have work and tasks to do as a part of being human, healing our family and elevating our experience until we return home to Him.. Like it or not these assignments belong to us! No one else can do them for us and deep inside we know this. We are responsible for our own happiness, our own healing and our own legacy.

Some of the assignments we take on are not from God. It's oftentime unnecessary worrying, unnecessary stressing. It's trying to belittle God! It shows up as listening to others or trying to live up to some expectation that was not from God. As you see, each of these ladies had assignments and through these undertakings they gained wisdom that they shared from completing the assignments. They lean on and trust in God! So they were able to extract the positive, the knowledge, the lesson, the healing, and the vulnerability.

How we navigate our journeys was not perfect or always Christian aligned but it was divine. So,be advised that healing has some drama in it and we must determine a sense of resolution or conclusion for ourselves, regardless of how others may feel, knowing that everyone has the right to their process even if their point of view is different from ours. So, What is your assignment? Let us begin!

www.ingramcontent.com/pod-product-compliance
Lightning Source LLC
Chambersburg PA
CBHW050847260726
48660CB00006B/2485